"For years I've loved and admired the work of Wayne Karlin. There is no other American novelist quite like him."—Gloria Emerson

"His work offers global meaning and a strong sense of purpose... in light of slavery, the Holocaust, and all these wars where Johnny had to carry a gun in order to survive, Karlin and Curbstone clearly do us all some good. They know it is the words—the essential element of open dialogue, the bare bones of human expression—that finally treat these old wounds and forever change the mythology of war." — Ricardo Cortez Cruz, *American Book Review*

**On *Rumors and Stones* (1996):**
"For the sake of humanity, we need to read Wayne Karlin on war and peace. Studying the holocaust of his immediate forebears and the Viet Nam/American War of his own experience, he has written a life-saving book."—Maxine Hong Kingston

"A gem of a book burnished with poetic language and images."—*Baltimore Jewish Times*

"Karlin's deft melding of disparate narratives will stand as a unique and valuable addition to the literature of the Holocaust."—*Washington Post Book World*

**On *Prisoners* (1998):**
"Karlin is one of the most gifted, passionate, and powerful writers of his generation."—George Garrett, in choosing *Prisoners* as one of the most notable books of 1998 in the *Dictionary of Literary Biography*

"*Prisoners* is superb. The reader is drawn into this powerful, richly layered novel by the poetic language, the compelling stories, and the wide-ranging themes. Ultimately we realize the various ways we are all prisoners of war."—Bobbie Ann Mason

"In *Prisoners*, [Karlin] examines war and race, blood and bones in a story linking several wars and the painful trail of memory...poetic, powerful fiction."—Mary Ann Carroll, *Booklist*

"*Prisoners* is an intense, short novel spanning continents east and west, centuries past and present. Mr. Karlin's writing is superb."—*The Asian Reporter*

"It is literature that allows writers—and readers—to follow the emotional shrapnel, if you will, of the Vietnam War as it sprayed across the lives of Vietnamese and Americans who battled there and across all the other lives of those who were touched... Karlin, who has written frequently on Vietnam, brilliantly layers in the American context."—Lisa See, *San Jose Mercury News*

"Though...more books have been written about Vietnam than any other war..., Karlin moves himself into the upper echelon of this vast list of authors with this story of Kiet-Keisha. In terms of giving authentic, literary substance, he belongs with the other giants of his genre...Moreover, his prose is as richly poetic and resonating as Walt Whitman..."—*American Book Review*

**On *The Wished-for Country* (2002):**
"...a powerful story. Karlin has chronicled a part of our history that is all too often ignored, and given voice to people who are usually left mute."—*The Washington Post*

"In *The Wished-for Country*, Karlin goes beyond the genteel world depicted in most colonial novels to create a riveting stage for his unusual, terrifying passion play."—*Publishers Weekly*

" The book delivers. It is a worthy conceit—using separate voices enunciate ever-current issues of birth, race, gender, class, greed, education, along with a healthy genuflection to environment and geography."—*The Baltimore Sun*

"Like Cormac McCarthy's unremittingly bloody meridians, Karlin's *The Wished-for Country* is equally riveting, unsettlingly violent, and breathtakingly vivid."—*The Bloomsbury Review*

# WAR MOVIES

## Journeys to Vietnam: Scenes and Out-takes

by
WAYNE KARLIN

Curbstone Press

printed in Canada on acid-free paper by Best Book / Transcontinental
Cover design: Les Kanturek

Front cover photos reprinted courtesy of Mega Media Pte Ltd &
Vietnam Media Corporation, and Wayne Karlin.

NATIONAL
ENDOWMENT
FOR THE ARTS

This book was published with the support
of the Connecticut Commission on Culture
and Tourism, the National Endowment for
the Arts, and donations from many
individuals. We are very grateful for this
support.

Library of Congress Cataloging-in-Publication Data

Karlin, Wayne.
    War movies : scenes and out-takes / by Wayne Karlin.— 1st ed.
       p. cm.
    Includes bibliographical references and index.
    ISBN 1-931896-16-X (pbk. : acid-free paper)
    1. Karlin, Wayne—Travel—Vietnam. 2. Screenwriters—United
States—Biography. 3. Vietnamese Conflict, 1961-1975—Veterans—
United States—Biography. 4. Vietnamese Conflict, 1961-1975 Motion
pictures and the confict. 5. Vietnam—Description and travel. 6.
Vietnam—In motion pictures. 7. Americans—Vietnam. I. Title.
    PS3561.A625Z477 2005
    818'.5403—dc22                                    2004029793

published by
CURBSTONE PRESS   321 Jackson St.   Willimantic, CT 06226
        phone: 860-423-5110    e-mail: info@curbstone.org
                    www.curbstone.org

*In loving memory of Gloria Emerson*

Portions of this book, in different forms, were published in *Free Fire Zone: Short Stories by Vietnam Veterans; Manoa: A Pacific Journal of International Writing; Michigan Quarterly Review; North American Review; Nimrod: An International Journal; Tuoi Tre (Youth Magazine of Ho Chi Minh City, in translation); War, Literature and the Arts: An International Journal;* and *The Washington Post.*

For Le Minh Khue, Ho Anh Thai, Phan Thanh Hao, Tran Van Thuy, Judd Ne'eman, Nguyen Phan Quang Binh, Ngo Thi Bich Hanh, Jonathan Foo, and Adam, my companions on this road, and for Ohnmar, companion on all roads.

I am grateful to the Maryland State Arts Commission and the National Endowment for the Arts for their support.

Excerpts from *Khe Sanh Hill Fights of 1967* reprinted with the permission of Ray Stubbe.

"Letter" is reprinted from *Beautiful Wreckage: New & Selected Poems*, W.D. Ehrhart, Adastra Press, 1999, by permission of the author.

Excerpt from "Revelation in the Mother Lode", page 42, reprinted with the permission of George Evans.

**Out-take, n.** 1. a scene, or take, photographed or taped for a film or TV program, but not included in the shown version. 2. a defective recording of music, etc., not used for commercial release.

"Coppola makes his film like the Americans made war—in this sense, it is the best possible testimonial —with the same immoderation, the same excess of means, the same monstrous candor...and the same success...the war as entrenchment, as technological and psychedelic fantasy, the war as a succession of special effects, the war become film even before being filmed."—Jean Baudrillard

# SCENE ONE
## In-Flight Movies:
## 2000

*Out-take: Medevac*

*Standing by for missions, he always has the feeling he is being centered in the lens of a movie camera. Flight suit and sunglasses, focused in sharply by the magnifying clearness of the Danang air. A loud buzzer sounds with dramatic insistence. A long shot: the crews running self-consciously to the helicopters, loading machine guns competently, talking flight talk, sticking their thumbs up. Switch to the interior of the helicopter; the lens zooms in for a really fine shot of his sweaty, grease-stained face framed over his machine gun by the open port. Then a full shot of the interior: the black crew-chief pumping the A.P.E, then running forward to his gun, black and white at the opposite ports, the subtle impact of the scene: no racists in foxholes, by God.*

*The sun sinks as the helicopter rises. The gunner looks at its fall and feels powerful and full of height. In its wake, the sun begins sucking the colors out of the ground, and the earth seems insignificant to him.*

*The crew talks on the intercom, the cords on their helmets and their voices linking them in the darkness. They are flying towards Dong Ha. Hastily to Hastings, the gunner thinks. Operation Hastings. Where did they get the names? He is trying to slide his sight through the darkness, looking for flashes, for tracers, for anything. For today's trick we will clear the DMZ with Norman cavalrymen. They must be catching shit, he thinks, to be calling for planes on secondary alert. Means the choppers already at Dong Ha are very full, and the crews will be cleaning out the insides with hoses,*

3

*washing away any spare bleeding parts left sticking on the helicopters' decks.*

*The trap door of a gallows suddenly opens, right at the moment when he is counting on more time. A drop and a wait for the noose to snap his neck.*

*The helicopter falls, then seems to catch itself and circle down more lazily. Leaning out of his port, he can see the flashes of the strobe the grunts are using to mark the landing zone, but the light doesn't illuminate the terrain. The aircraft drops into darkness. The noose never tightens.*

*The helicopter lands hard and the rear ramp drops heavily. The gunner stays at his gun while the crew--chief runs back to help with the wounded. Looking over the barrel, he can just make out part of the circle of infantrymen around the Zone. Their green backs look tense and they are mud-spattered and somehow fragile-looking in their hardness. They don't look as if they'd stepped off a tapestry. Backs and saggy asses and legs and boots. Too normal for Normans.*

*The wounded come through the open rear hatch, touching the sides of the helicopter with gentle, bloody hands. They are already a race apart, consecrated in the eyes of the unwounded, receivers of blows meant for the unhurt. Some intact Marines are carrying those unable to walk and laying them out on the deck. The helicopter is filling up and its blades beat the air insistently as if feeling the danger and straining to go. The wounded are twisted into one another, holding onto each other, softly bleeding into each other's wounds. The gunner strains for comparisons, sees a pile of soiled laundry, cloth arms and legs locked into impossible positions. Or pudding. Bleeding pudding. Hastings pudding.*

*The ramp closes and the helicopter lifts. A corpsman moves among the Marines, shooting morphine into them. Many haven't been treated at all yet. We must have landed right in the middle of something, the gunner thinks.*

*A Marine, his torn trousers showing shredded meat, is trying to stand up next to the gunner, leaving more room for the worse wounded. He puts his hand on the gunner's shoulder to steady himself, then looks at him apologetically. The gunner turns away for a second, and notices the black man lying near his feet. The man seems to have a red gelatinous mass growing from the side of his neck, twisting his head and strangling him. His eyes bulge.*

*All this in a second, a split second, for he is dutifully looking out of the port and doesn't miss the flashes below and the green tracers flying up at the helicopter. He fires his guilt down at the flashes and feels it leave him in violent spurts through the machine gun barrel. Just shooting at our noise, he thinks; they're too far. His own tracers flash red. Maybe I hit an NVA, he thinks, and he's being dragged off on a hook by his buddy. Who's feeling guilty the hook ain't in his own pudding neck. Fucking fool. The firing stops.*

*Then they are dropping towards Dong Ha, and are down, and the ramp drops again.*

*The corpsmen come in with some service troops who have volunteered to carry stretchers. See what they've been missing. The bearers are in respectful awe of the wounded, but try to act as nonchalant as the corpsmen. The walking wounded begin walking and the gunner helps the man who had been leaning next to him walk out, then turns back inside.*

*The corpsmen are going through the men lying on the deck, quickly, competently, placing two enchanted fingers on wrists, bestowing life or death. The stretcher bearers begin lifting one man; the corpsman is still touching his wrist. Save it, the corpsman advises, he's bought it. The dead man is a big blond boy.*

*"Save it," the economical corpsman says, and gestures impatiently at the volunteers. "Get'm out quick; he can't feel nothin'." One of the bearers grabs the man's ankles and drags the body out. The head bounces up and down on the ramp as the body slides, then thuds dully on the ground.*

*Save what? The gunner thinks.*

*He goes out and walks away from the fuel lines and tries to catch a quick smoke before they take off again.*

# IN-FLIGHT MOVIES

After I'd gotten through customs at Don Maung, I went out to the taxi queue in front of the terminal and gave the first driver the name of my hotel. I had a one night stopover in Bangkok before going on to Hanoi. The taxi sped down the elevated airport expressway, exited onto a side street that I knew would take us to Sukhumvit Road, then nudged itself into a slow stream of farting taxis, jitneys, Mercedes, and motorcycles. The city squeezed in on me. The driver began his litany. You want massage? You want a girl? A boy? Young? Old? Once, on another trip, I had been asked if I were a sadist. There was no leer, nothing judgmental about the question: the driver merely establishing what his potential market was, though at first I'd heard "dentist," which would involve a kind of perversity I couldn't begin to imagine. A what? You know, to hit, to whip. A sa-dist.

Oh. No, I'm a writer.

"The hotel's at Soi 11," I said to the driver's neck. It was the same place my travel agent had booked for me the last time I'd come to Bangkok; when I'd checked in then I'd realized, with no particular shock at the synchronicity, that I was two blocks from the hotel where I'd stayed when I'd first come to Bangkok on R&R, in 1966. We looped under the expressway, where it formed the cave-roof for a netherworld of stall-like bars, huddled in dusty pools of shadow, their interiors lit in a dim reddish glow that reflected against the underside of the road and turned the bar girls perched on their stools into caricatures of bar girls in a caricature of hell. Emerged into the blazing light again and began to inch up

6

Sukhumvit, past the Indian and Arab tailor shops, the crust of sidewalk stalls selling switch-blades, compasses, rolling suitcases and overnight bags, t-shirts, watches, brand-name counterfeits. Thai office workers, students and business people, cell phones clamped to their ears, walked by briskly, ignoring the old Western men, their faces chalky and cadaverous in the strong light, being led like the dead on leave by the teenaged whores whose arms encircled their waists. Two streams of existence twisting around each other, but as separate as if they moved in parallel dimensions. Soi Cowboy was outside my window now, lined with more open-air whore bars. I could glimpse the hotel where I'd spent my week off from the war. The city had grown up around it. The old men might have been representations of all those who hadn't. I felt suddenly trapped. As if I'd never left. The sensation I have from time to time that my life since the war is only a dream I'm having during the war. Of all the places to spend the night, I told myself. I should have just stayed in the airport.

We stopped dead, the traffic clotting into a solid mass. I looked out at the sidewalk.

The woman stood in the classic stance, one hip thrust out, a hand splayed on it. Probably too old for the bars or massage parlors. A veteran. She was wearing what seemed a green jacket-tunic from a businesswoman suit, but only the tunic, her hand sliding the bottom edge up an inch or so to show stained buttocks. It was her only movement. She stood still as an exhibit representing something I felt too tired to learn, or re-learn, next to an overflowing trash barrel. Staring unblinking at the motionless vehicles that stood like other exhibits, post-apocalyptic statuary, her eyes so void of light or life they could have been painted on her skin. Then she moved over a foot or two, into the exact same stance. She was parallel to my window. If I met her eyes, two vacuums would meet, form some vortex that would suck us both in.

A teenaged Thai girl walked by, stopped, and grinned

incredulously at the sight of the whore. She was slim and beautiful and wore every ripped-off brand name stacked on the tables that lined Sukhumvit Road like altars in a cargo cult: Guess t-shirt, Gucci belt, tight Klein jeans. Though they may have been, for all I knew, the real items, the girl a child of privilege, just back from four years of polishing and globalization at Sarah Lawrence or Smith. I felt a sudden and irrational surge of anger at her innocence, at her arrogance, and then, as I sat insulated and air-conditioned behind the closed window, at my own.

Still smiling, the girl suddenly began circling the whore, bringing her face close, drawing it back, some snake dance. Laughing out loud. I waited for the older woman to reach behind, draw a razor from her hair. But she stood as before, indifferent, looking through the kid. The girl danced up to the garbage bin. Began rummaging inside it, throwing trash on the sidewalk, drawing out a plastic bag that looked like a removed breast implant, its bottom sagged and heavy with some brackish yellow liquid, a straw sticking out of its bunched top. The girl put the straw to her mouth and began sucking in the liquid. Cheeks going hollow. Her hands were powdered with dust. Looking closer, I could see that her hair was caked with filth, her pupils dilated. She looked quite mad. When she opened her mouth, I saw blackened stubs. I saw a face from a story the man sitting next to me on the first leg of the flight here had put into my mind, a vengeful wraith come howling out of the past, out of the door of my R&R hotel, the zombie-hollow remains of all the women's bodies we'd filled with ourselves in order to know we could still feel something, that we were still alive. She continued to dance around the whore, the whore's stillness suddenly part of the choreography, a pivot, and all of it framed and somehow focused by the window through which I stared. And then, suddenly, so was I, as trapped in some internal dance as she was, flapping in helpless circles.

"How long you stay in Bangkok?" the driver asked me.

"Just a day. I'm going to Vietnam."

His eyes, in the rearview mirror, widened, as if in disbelief. "What for, man?"

"Working on a movie."

He grinned and nodded, as if that made everything all right.

\*\*\*

Time always cracked and spilled odd bits and pieces of the past into the present whenever I traveled to Vietnam, as if I was violating a law of nature by going back. Returning seemed to link and magnetize some scatter of debris in my soul that drew charged, serendipitous situations and people to me like filings. As if it was all happening to teach me something. A dangerous notion to carry around in one's head when it was connected to Vietnam. Especially for the Vietnamese.

I was on my way this time to work on a movie, a joint Vietnamese-Singaporean film about the war called *Song of the Stork*. The day before, after I'd checked in for the flight that would take me to Los Angeles, where I'd catch another flight to Bangkok and yet another to Hanoi, the airport p.a. suddenly stopped informing me that my unattended bags would be disintegrated and began crackling words I couldn't be sure weren't echoing only in my mind: "Will passenger Nguyen Ky please come to the ticket counter." The request was repeated until my flight was called for boarding, the name of the Prime Minister of South Vietnam when I was in Vietnam chanted over and over, like an insistent nudge from my memory, calling up the slim playboy in his purple scarf, black, tailored flight-suit, his female clone, in identical flight suit and Ray-Bans, stapled to his arm. I suppose the person being paged could actually have been Nguyen Cao Ky. It was altogether possible he was passing through or living in Washington: the city was rimed with layers of leftover Cold

War archaeology. I had never actually seen the man or his wife in the flesh, only their images in magazines and on posters that the Ruff Puffs, South Vietnamese home militia, would fasten to the walls of schools and pagodas in the villages near our perimeter. The villagers would look through the posters as if they weren't there, the same way they looked at us. Often the posters were torn down at night, though once I noticed one that had been soaked with urine, Ky's face pissed out, the walls dripping. From the amount of piss, the activity seemed communal. It also seemed a particularly dedicated act, to piss that high, especially for short people like the Vietnamese.

I was thinking of Ky as I boarded the plane and walked down the aisle to my seat. When I found it and settled in, I nodded to the man in the next seat. He nodded back, sighed, and slipped a book into the pouch net in front of him, then closed his eyes. My gaze went to the title showing above the lip of the pouch: *About Face: the Odyssey of an American Warrior,* ex-colonel David Hackworth's memoir. Something like excitement or dread or both stirred in my stomach. I wasn't sure what to call the feeling, only that I knew, more than getting on the plane, the succession of coincidences— Ky and now this—signaled the true beginning of the trip.

I eye-balled the man furtively. He was the right age, close-cropped hair, white short-sleeved shirt, a slight paunch. A double-dipper with a service pension and a civil service or contractor's job, something technical. I thought of saying something about the Hackworth book—I'd read it, liked it— but stopped myself. The man, given age, appearance, choice of reading material, had to be a vet, or a wannabe, and one was never sure what directions such conversations could take. In fact, at second look, he resembled a boy from North Carolina, from race-car driver Richard Petty's town, Randall, whom I had known in the Marines—or at least he looked the way I imagined that boy would look if he'd made it to middle-age.

I glanced at the screen on the bulkhead in front of the center rows of seats. A camera mounted on the front of the plane gave me the runway rushing under us, dropping off, the real estate developments and corporate Chichen Itzas of Northern Virginia miniaturizing, then vaporized by clouds. I looked away, my stomach lurching. Dozed. When I awoke, the screen showed our position on a map: somewhere over the Great Lakes. If I stared at it, I was sure, we would remain frozen in place. The watched kettle. An attendant walked down the aisle, offering headphones. I declined. The man next to me said, "no thanks," and pulled the book from its pouch, clicking on the overhead light. Its beam fell on the pages. I gave up. The book seemed to demand acknowledgement, a nod towards its link with my destination.

"Good book," I muttered.

"It's like he put into words all the ways I felt about the war," the man said slowly. "Makes me remember how very screwed up it really was."

I nodded slowly. "I know what you mean."

He looked at me. "You were there," he pronounced.

The lights were suddenly switched off. The attendant began lowering the window shades. We exchanged a litany of place names and dates, like a ceremonial chant whose ending would reveal our secret and true names. Or like two dogs sniffing each other, he might have said; he had been, it turned out, in a dog handlers' platoon in the First Air Cavalry. Was now—I'd been right—a military contractor, worked at a California Naval facility.

I let myself relax, turn off. I knew what I'd hear now; had talked to other dog handlers. Poignant stories of animal devotion, the dog that sacrificed its life to save the G.I. like a canine embodiment of the Noble Cause itself.

"I'm a little surprised at myself," the man said. "I never talk about it."

"Why's that?"

"People usually don't want to hear it the way I remember it. They want it the way it was supposed to be."

We slowly turned away from each other and stared at the silent images on the screen in the bulkhead above the seats: astronauts on some ill-fated mission to Mars. Gary Sinese was yelling something to an actor I couldn't place, frantically punching glowing buttons on a panel, nothing responding, flashing lights, everything out of control.

"How was it supposed to be?" I asked.

"Oh, you know," he eyed me uneasily, leaned forward. "How bad it was for us, and the hero stuff. The war movie stuff. Don't get me wrong. We were crazy brave; you know that. Out on point, with the dogs. I lost friends, human and dog. I hated it—never wanted to be there in the first place, but I got out there, did my job. But it's the way we treated the Vietnamese that sticks to me. The murders and rapes. That's why I stopped talking to people—even the guys who were there don't want to remember that stuff. Some of the handlers would set their dogs loose on caged prisoners, tear them to pieces. Guys, when we went on sweeps, would sometimes grab a girl from the villages, rape them. Nobody stopped them. You know, it was all sexual, that was the thing I came to realize, part of the way we were trained to look at women. All of it was sex gone bad."

I looked at him.

"There was a girl I remember," the man started.

*People usually don't want to hear it the way I remember it.* What came to me, as he told his unexpected war story, was how even my own memories would fork into two streams, intertwining but moving in different directions. The war movie stuff. And the other stuff. The first urban legends about the Vietnam war had been that it was all atrocity; we were all baby killers. Now nobody was; we were all broken but noble warriors, spit on by apocryphal hordes of demonstrators; we were all there building orphanages (never mind who was populating them) and there were no American atrocities, except for the aberration, caused by one nutty Lieutenant, of My Lai, and a few years later John Kerry, running for President, would be lambasted for having once said there were any atrocities at all committed by American troops. You couldn't have it both ways. I understood the temptation. What I wanted to recall was working in the villes, winning hearts and minds on Civic Action patrols, later, flying gunner on re-supplies, inserts, extracts, rescues and medical evacuations. I wanted to focus on the compassion of the corpsmen, the courage of the air crews, the occasional glimpse of true self-sacrifice and nobility. There was Calley but there was also Mike Clausen, a helicopter crew chief in my unit—though not while I was in it—who won a Medal of Honor by running into a minefield to guide and carry wounded and dead Marines to his helicopter. People forgot or didn't know about that either. Who wanted to think about the other stuff? Maybe it hadn't happened. Or if it did, it was part of our victimization. All the kids there were armed with exploding shoeshine boxes, weren't they? Millions of them— a nation of exploding shoeshine boys. Anyway, we were just kids ourselves. People had given their lives or their bodies to help save other people. The other memories only stained that. How could I denigrate their sacrifices? How could I denigrate the sacrifices of their dogs?

The dog-handler had been there in sixty-nine: my tour was sixty-six, sixty-seven. It had seemed an easier time, at least in terms of moral ambiguity. Most of the missions I'd flown on as a helicopter gunner were to protect or extract or to rescue. I hadn't seen what he'd described. Yet I could supply the roots and context for his peculiar dog stories from my own memories, and if I focused on them they always developed slowly into the specific images of a boy in a foxhole near Ky Ha displaying to me, like his calling card, a Polaroid of a mangled column of dead women and children he and his squad had ambushed on their way to market, of other boys chucking scrap wood from the back of a six-by truck at people on bicycles, of helicopter pilots talking casually of wiping out any village they took fire from, of a deadly and prevalent contempt for the people we were supposedly there to save from themselves. Seeing every South Vietnamese as contemptuous or deadly created a certain ambience that I'd remember again months later when I heard about former Nebraska governor and senator Bob Kerrey, also a Medal of Honor winner, rounding up and shooting villagers, slitting the throats of some grandparents and their grandchildren whose only crime was being in their house—that is, of being Vietnamese in Vietnam. A story I couldn't listen to without thinking of the line in the old Gene Wilder, Richard Pryor film: Why did you kill the family? Because they were home.

But it was a story Kerrey would deny, in spite of the witnesses to it; his memory was confused, he said.

My seat mate's wasn't. "We lost the war," he was saying, as we both kept our eyes fixed on the nearly human face of an edifice the astronauts had discovered on the red surface of Mars, "when we started killing everybody."

It was as succinct and accurate a summary as I had ever heard expressed both of the war and what the term "lost" really meant, and I found myself touched, deeply, that this man who looked like, and in fact was, a military base-town Rotarian, who worked in a milieu that would make it both easy and desirable to revise his memories, who looked like, in fact, a friend of my youth grown wise, had held that sharp-edged truth hard against his heart.

"What's your name?" I asked.

"Forrest," the man said, extending his hand.

I shook it, smiling. "Gump?"

But the man didn't smile back, hadn't seen the movie. *Forrest Gump.* A film about as real as a space voyage to a monument built on Mars by wise aliens: Vietnam presented without Vietnamese, a landscape that existed only as backdrop, a way for America to find out things about itself.

Presumably that it was as innocent as an idiot. Now, with Sinese, another figure from *Gump* playing on the screen in front of us—his character journeying once again to a planet he'd assumed to be empty of conscious life, only to find it was inhabited and had its own agenda—I suddenly felt I was sitting with the reverse Forrest. An aware, intelligent anti-Gump who'd refused the brightly-wrapped box filled with sweet little dollops of chocolate, presented as palatable truths.

I asked him if he'd seen any of the other Vietnam movies.

"The only one that was anything like I remember it was *Platoon*," he said. "Maybe because Stone was a grunt. Or maybe because it showed some of the things happening to the Vietnamese. But usually I don't watch the Vietnam war movies." He grinned at me. "I prefer *South Pacific*."

I nodded. I'd been thinking quite a bit about war movies since I'd found, to my surprise, that I'd be working on one. A few weeks before I'd gotten on this flight, I'd had an argument about *Platoon* with my friend Bill Ehrhart, a writer and combat veteran. I'd liked the film, I told Ehrhart: in spite of the hokey biblical allegories and nomenclature, Elias, Barnes, Chris and the gang struggling with their capacity for doing great good and great evil seemed a realistic way to depict a war in which altruism and heroism, brutality and murder were so inextricably intertwined. But Ehrhart had been vehement "I hate Hollywood," he said. "All movies about the war are bad. Not just *Rambo*. Even the so-called anti-war films like *Platoon* glamorize it, make kids want to experience it. Charlie Sheen doing John Wayne doing Audie Murphy. The hero suffers and learns bad stuff about himself and the world and comes back with sexy mysteries in his eyes. Plus he gets to shoot a lot of nifty guns. All with haunting background music. But it's not just that. The thing is, the movies make it desirable, just because they're *movies*." His voice had risen as he spoke; by the end of it he seemed enraged. They were all the same, he'd said. Old Joe Campbell. The hero leaves his safe place, goes to a dark place of demons and ashes, meets questionable guides, receives a wound, achieves the obligatory homecoming, brings his newly achieved wisdom to the eagerly waiting community. Obligatory baptisms of fire, obligatory sex scenes with nurturing and/or treacherous Oriental women, obligatory wounds of body and/or soul.

I had understood Ehrhart's anger, his fear of the inevitable flattening to fit comfortable perceptions and patterns that were, after all, what sold stuff. But at the same time I had liked *Platoon*, partially, perversely, because the film had become emblematic, to those veterans and politicians who were rewriting the war as Noble Cause, of everything Hollywood got wrong about the Vietnam war. It had become the film to be hated for anyone who didn't want to remember or see what Forrest remembered, who wanted to leave out what Forrest couldn't forget. Who only wanted John Wayne. Fleshy, florid Marion Morrison, who'd never spent a day in a uniform that didn't come from a prop department, who in *The Green Berets* had defended Fort Vietnam as if it were Fort Apache. Who'd been the icon we'd carried with us to boot camp, and later in infantry training, when the pop-up target, shoot-from-your-hip course was called the John Wayne, and he was the figure you measured yourself against, the father you saw yourself pleasing through imitation.

Before I'd left, I'd also read an article about Mel Gibson making a movie about the battle of Ia Drang that would show the heroism of American soldiers in Vietnam, and would also try to humanize the Vietnamese enemy. Both good things to do, I'd thought. The men at Ia Drang had been heroic. One was now a neighbor of mine in Maryland, also, as it were, a man named Forrest. He'd saved his entire company by running back through a gauntlet of enemy fire to take command. But two things had disturbed me about the article. Its author, also a Vietnam veteran, had asked Oliver Stone for his reaction, and Stone said that he was afraid it would be

a John Wayne type movie. "We should be so lucky," the writer
had responded. He wanted John Wayne. He was tired, he
wrote, of seeing his war portrayed in movies such as *Platoon*,
as an imperialist, racist venture. We'd been there, he
contended, to bring freedom to the South Vietnamese, but
you never saw that, or the heroism of Americans at battles
like Ia Drang. Now Gibson would give it to us, or at least
give us the first part of the battle when G.I.'s had held off and
killed thousands of the enemy. It was the other thing that had
bothered me. The second half of the fight at Ia Drang, a
disaster for the Americans, when the enemy ambushed and
nearly wiped out a battalion, the part of the battle my
neighbor George Forrest was in, apparently would be left out
of the movie. Just as Gibson had left out or reversed a few
troublesome details about the institution of slavery from his
epic about the American revolution, *The Patriot*. As (the
writer of the article seemed to gratefully assume), he would
leave out any other troubling ambiguities about a war in
which many Vietnamese, in fact, saw us as redcoats to their
Minutemen. John Wayne didn't allow any ambiguities. John
Wayne said you couldn't have Ia Drang and My Lai in the
same war. You could have *We Were Soldiers* and the upright
Colonel Moore, or you could have *Platoon,* and the terrible
Sgt. Barnes. But you couldn't have both. In the mythologizing
of war, the first casualty was the ability to accept moral
complexity, and by the next year, when the movie I was going
to now was finished, that concept itself would finally be
buried under the rubble of the World Trade Center, and the
world presented to us as a place of stark evil or pure good,
just as it had been before our war melted both together, like
the flesh of enemies sealed by the same wash of fire.

Not that conveniently reshaped memory was only an
American disease. One of the Vietnamese writers I'd worked
with, a People's Army veteran named Vu Bao, wrote a short
story about a battle in which one man is a coward, refuses to
advance under fire, wets himself. Yet when a documentary

film crew comes afterwards and asks the soldiers to reenact the battle, the coward, who happens to be photogenic, is chosen to be filmed raising a flag over an enemy bunker. Twenty years later, that scene, re-released in another foreign film, and reproduced on posters and postage stamps, has become the official memory of the battle. The veterans who were there resent it, but are told to be quiet. The real account would be socially inconvenient. It wouldn't be what it was supposed to be.

What had outraged Vu Bao was what had also outraged Ehrhart. The Thing that we knew would eventually swallow all of us. Neither the written word nor the real world itself could compete against the seductive, shaping power of the magnified image on the screen. The words and memories of the Forrest who sat next to me couldn't compete against the computer-generated revisions of history in *Forrest Gump*. Like many writers, I was used to people who had read one or another of my books asking me, "When are they going to make a movie of this?" As if what I'd written could only bloom in that way. And I was aware that often I felt the same way they did. Since the late seventies, I'd always felt obligated to see the Vietnam war films that came out, as if in some way they finally legitimized not the reasons for the war but its very existence, and so, pathetically enough, my own. People didn't know what they were to think of the war until they saw it on the screen. They didn't know if they should think about it at all. It was the patent wisdom that had pasted a leering grin on the face of my taxi driver in Bangkok. Nothing was real until it was a movie.

I stared at the screen and then glanced at Forrest. What if I were going back to Vietnam to make his movie instead? What would his movie, his interior *South Pacific*, be, if we were to make it instead of *Stork,* make *Forrest* without *Gump*? If we were to stream back in all the grim out-takes, the missing left behind in the landing zone, abandoned in the name of comfort and convenience, but still festering in some dark cell of memory. Set it into the framing rectangle above the seats, pulsing now with senseless, disconnected shapes, visual echoes from the seethe in his brain.

*The girl huddles in the shadows, as far to the back of the cage as she can get, curled around herself, clutching her knees to her chest. A configuration that breaks the dog-handler's heart, calls to him the position his dog, Chance, would take, when it slept in the curl of his master's body whenever they could sleep, out in the field, the dog moaning and twitching with nightmares that would leak into the soldier's own dreams—human throats under his teeth, the flash and ear-splitting roar of a booby-trap. The two American interrogators—Rodgers and Hammerstein, the dog-handler calls them—joking with the two ARVN interrogators. All four wearing wrap-around sun-glasses. The two Americans beefy, pasty-faced; their jobs have kept them out of the bush. The ARVN in tailored tiger-stripped fatigues, the trousers skin-tight and tapered, their thighs and calves identical in diameter so their legs seem like two sticks stuck into their polished boots.*

*A fecal stink suddenly wafts from the cage, the girl defecating in fear. The men laugh and the two dogs Rodgers and Hammerstein are holding tight on their chains snarl and strain. For some reason—perhaps the names he has given the two American interrogators—the soldier begins to think of South Pacific. He had loved the musical when he was in high school. It had been one of the reasons he had come to the war. The movie; he'd never seen it on stage. Staring open-mouthed, in a theatre in Greensboro, so that Laurie, his girl, looked at him and shook him, as if suddenly afraid. The opening scene: the lush greenery, the brown-skinned natives waking gracefully under swaying palms, had evoked the world that waited outside, a possibility beyond Randall, North Carolina, home of NASCAR champ Richard Petty himself, the smug assumption he saw all around him that this was the only world, the inevitable trajectory of girl,*

*football, state college, wife, factory—floor or management.
Aware also, by the time Mary Martin burst into You've Got to
be Carefully Taught, of where he was, specifically in this seat,
in this theatre, the white faces around him, hearing for the
first time in his life the whispers coming from that dark
balcony that hung over his head.*

*The girl in the film, he realizes suddenly, Marine
Lieutenant Joe Cable's girl, his love, the one his heart called
him to but his prejudice kept him from, was Vietnamese. It hit
the handler like a hammer. Liat. Tonkinese, they'd said in the
movie. But that was the same thing. Liat. Of course. He thinks
of silent Liat as he stares at the girl in the cage, her flanks
stained by her own shit, her hands trembling as she clutches
her knees to her chest. She'd remained silent under the
interrogation; screamed when the electricity had shattered
her nipples and vagina; gagged when the water had been
forced down her throat, moaned when she was hoisted from
the rafter, arms behind her. But had said nothing they'd
wanted to hear. Refused to tell them what they wanted to hear.
Silent Liat, he thinks. He had loved her, in the movie; thought
Lt. Joe Cable a fool. She drove Laurie right out of his mind
and later that night, Laurie's head bobbing over him in the
front seat, the hair he had pressed down was Liat's, and he
didn't give a big rat's ass if Laurie was dreaming her lips
around old Richard Petty's gearshift. Liat. She had been silent
in the movie too. Silent and smiling, undressing within
minutes of being introduced to him by her mother, doing
whatever Lieutenant Cable wanted. In love with him just
because he was Lieutenant Cable and she was just Liat.
Because she was cute and Tonkinese. Telling him what he
wanted to hear. Happy talky talky, happy talk.*

*Her mother, he thinks, feeling feverish. Bloody Mary. He
had loved Bloody Mary also. Happy, entrepreneurial Bloody
Mary. Pimping her daughter to the lieutenant, because he
was white and powerful. Pimping her to underscore the great
lesson of tolerance that made people in that Greensboro*

*theatre uncomfortable, that stirred a wake of mutters and curses and shuffles as people got up and left the white seats. You've got to be carefully taught, Lieutenant Cable sings, squinting his eyes, pressing down on her shining waterfall of black hair. Shit fire, the old bitch was pimping her daughter, the handler thinks, as he watches Rodgers and Hammerstein let the dogs loose on Liat.*

There it was. Maybe we all needed a movie, needed to stain ourselves onto the blankness. It had always been cinematic anyway. When I'd started writing some scenes for *Song of the Stork* that would involve a young American G.I., I tried to refresh my memory for details by looking at several short stories I'd written just after coming back from the war, stories that in essence had become my memories. I was not really surprised to see how much they reflected that sense we'd had of playing roles in a movie unreeling in our minds. It had been like that even then, even as it was happening, and those stories seeped back in again, as I worked on this book, on the movie. The movie I was working on and the movie I'd once been in. Somehow it had all melded together.

SCENE TWO
The Storage Room:
2000

# THE STORAGE ROOM

As it does a few days later, the country of the war passing by outside the bus windows in a succession of framed scenes from memories that seam into cuts from the film we are making. Visible waves of heat, emerald rice paddies gridded by raised earth berms, boys with branch switches wading next to massive, mud-caked water buffaloes. In the prop bus behind us are stacked metal trunks full of equipment and uniforms: abandoned American M-16s and web gear and flak jackets and jungle utilities co-existing with North Vietnamese Army uniforms and AK-47s and Ho Chi Minh sandals made from rubber tires. The young Vietnamese woman sitting across from me is wearing a baseball hat emblazoned with a Nike swoosh. I ask her what the war means to her. She gives me the strained smile and stare of a student looking at her teacher and trying to figure out which answer he wants to hear.

"It's just history," she says, shrugging. She looks at me. "Anyway, the way they teach it is crap."

I'm not surprised at her words: many of the young people I met in Vietnam spoke with a selective openness that wouldn't have been possible a decade before. That they took for granted they could do so perhaps demonstrated the upside of forgetting one's history.

"Was anyone in your family a soldier?"

"Yes, my father."

"Was he hurt?"

For a moment, she stares at me, as if surprised I'm asking a question whose answer seems so obvious.

"Yes."

"How?"

"He was shot, several times. His health is still bad—he has problems because of this." She holds my gaze, then looks away. "But I'm not sure who shot him. It happened over thirty-five years ago," she says. "I guess the Americans or the French—which would it be at that time?"

"Doesn't he ever talk about it with you?"

Her eyes widen. "No, of course not," she says, as if I'd suggested incest.

Her words, her wince, the thought of her silent father, bring my mind back to the metal trunks, their lids tightly shut over other untold stories. I'd helped pick out the gear that had gone into those boxes, all of it kept in the storage room of the building the company was renting for its offices. The day before, two of the prop women had taken me up to the room. The silence as we came in seemed abrupt; I'd had the sense one sometimes gets, upon entering a space filled with very old things, of having interrupted a furtive, urgent conversation. Uniforms and fatigues hung limply from bars on metal frame racks, casting distorted black shadows over the concrete floor. Stacked against the walls and piled on the floor were American web belts, canteens, entrenching tool cases, magazine pouches, flak jackets, G.I. helmets and liners. The film people had gotten everything from the People's Army. I tried not to think about where and how that army had gotten it in the first place. I had complained to Binh and Jonathan, the Vietnamese and Singaporean co-directors, that the Vietnamese war films were always inaccurate about American uniforms and equipment, and I could see in the storage room that many of the utilities—fatigues—were, in fact, wrong: they were stateside issue, some with a hodgepodge of unit patches and ranks that must have been sewn on sleeves and collars by the prop ladies: a Big Red One patch on a shirt with USMC on the breast pocket and a Military Police patch on the collar, another shirt with captain's bars on one collar, black metal Marine Lance Corporal insignia on the other. Mixed with the rest though were worn-down green canvas and leather jungle boots and sets of jungle fatigues, ripped, sweat-stained, and faded, pouched with the big pockets on thighs and legs that had suddenly become fashionable in the States the year before. Expeditionary chic. I pulled these from the rest, the wannabe fatigues, tossed them into a pile: cloth arms and legs entwined. The cloth felt warm under my fingers. Some shirts still had the names of the boys who had worn them sewn above the breast pockets. I felt something tight and hot in my chest. Or became aware that it was there. Storage. Stored rage. The M-16s were stamped "Property of U.S. Government." I wanted, needed, to think that all this had come from the supplies left behind after '75.

I asked the women for a felt-tip marker, and then graffitied the helmet covers with whatever Vietnam talk came into my head. *Light My Fire. Short Time. You Don't See Me.* On the last one I scrawled *I'm Not Here.*

In the beginning, I'd been hesitant about becoming involved with the film. I already had a project with Vietnamese writers that was eating up my life, keeping me, my wife and son felt, unhealthily moored in the war.

What moored me though were not memories of the war, but the country itself. I'd made my first trip back in 1994, and returned nearly every year since. The earth-and-flesh reality of Vietnam, its stubborn, proven insistence on being itself, was somehow an antidote to the feeling of slippage that at times seized me in the middle years of my American life: the sense that my past, the common history I'd touched, was constantly being scripted to the needs of the moment. The country fastened me not to the war, but to my very life, in the sense one doesn't know what one has become until brought back to confront one's origins.

So I told myself. Yet I was here and not here, and there were other times I thought that edgy condition was the real country I sought. My work and friendships with the Vietnamese allowed me to be deeply part of something, and yet on its rim, the same position in fact I'd gravitated to in the war, when I'd been on the perimeter or helicopter crew, and since then as well: living in a rural area on the periphery of the capital city, teaching in a small college, taking on the small town role of cranky local writer. The hovering observer. You're a corner ghost, Phan Thanh Hao, the director's mother had told me: the invisible spirit that lives, noticing and unnoticed, in other people's houses. A description I liked, though I didn't know if I was meant to, or should.

The previous December, I'd sat in the home of Hao's son and daughter-in-law, Nguyen Phan Quang Binh and Ngo Thi Bich Hanh, with their two little girls on the couch next to me, doodling in their coloring books. It was a tall, narrow, old-style stone and brick Hanoi house, the last in an alley that ran off Ly Thuong Kiet, one of the main roads in town. We drank green tea and talked about movies. Binh had directed videos for MTV-Asia, and Hanh had produced commercials, but they wanted to do more now. Looking at them, I thought they seemed more like twins than husband and wife: of the same height, slim, their faces thin and intent, a gesture or word begun by one, finished by the other, their sentences alternating.

They wanted, Binh told me, to make a movie. *Song of the Stork* would be, Hanh said, the first film about the Vietnam-American war to be filmed on location in Vietnam, by and with Vietnamese. Though it would be a co-production, with a Singapore company. Jonathan Foo, Binh said. His wife, Peggy Lim, would co-produce, Hanh said. It would be, Binh said, their chance to tell the untold stories of the war. The war, Hanh said, that the American movies they had seen had left out.

I was half-listening, and somewhat defensive: Hao was a

good friend, and I liked Binh and Hanh, but I didn't know how seriously I should take them. Everyone wanted to make a movie. But even if they had the finances, the resources and the government permissions, it seemed a leap from the quick cuts, and flashy, self-referential images of music videos to a feature film with characters and a sustained story line.

"We want to do a real movie about the war," Binh said.

"You mean a movie about the real war."

"Yes," Hanh said, as if I had gotten it.

"O.K.," I'd said. "But it doesn't seem like a great leap. Every other movie I see when I turn on the TV is about the war."

"Yes," Binh said, "but you know, uncle, they are mostly very bad movies. And this is the first that will be done for international release, since we'll do it with the Singaporeans."

"And it is a, how did you say, very big leap for us," Hanh said.

The idea to do the film had come to them when they had done a music video and produced a concert with Jonathan and Peggy, and the two had asked them if they knew any actual VC. "As if the VC were still fighting in the jungle," Hanh said. "I told them: 'I'm VC; we're all VC here,' and they were very surprised."

The Singaporeans' curiosity had apparently legitimized the war as a subject for her and Binh. Until then, like the girl on the bus, they wanted to see it placed into the safety of history. Their elders never spoke of it, or rather only spoke of it in socially acceptable terms: a tedious lesson. It was tough to be the children of a mythological generation. The heroic sacrifices and solidarity of their parents were impossible to match and passé in any case, in the competitive market society Vietnam had become. No one wanted to think about it.

They, Binh and Hanh, probably knew very little about it themselves, I thought. Hanh had chided her Singaporean friends for their ignorance. But she didn't know that the term

"VC" was itself a derogatory American and South Vietnamese name for Vietnamese Communists that only applied to the Southern guerillas of the National Liberation Front, not the regular People's Army from the north in which her father had served. In which, in fact, he'd been a political commissar and an artillery officer, though I couldn't remember where.

"Where did your father fight?" I asked her.

"Mostly Quang Tri, I think," she said.

"I was there also."

"Yes," Binh said. "We know. That's why we want you. We don't want to repeat the way the American films, how would you say…?"

"Their self-centeredness."

"Yes. Their self-centeredness. The stories in the film will be about Vietnamese characters; some stories we already know from the war. But we want to have an American story as well. One in which the Americans are human."

"We have heard this one story," Hanh said, "about an American who sees a wounded Vietnamese soldier and who spares his life. He takes his diary, and looks at it, and then he doesn't shoot him or tell the others he, the Vietnamese, is still alive. Then after the war he finds him and returns the diary. Do you think this is a good story?"

I stared at them. We sat, the tiny tea cups frozen in our hands, the twin girls giggling over their books. What they seemed on the verge of offering me seemed unreal, as if I'd found myself in a constructed story, a plot that was bringing too many separate threads together. I shook my head. I could see my silence was making them uneasy.

"I don't think it's a very likely one. A soldier wouldn't leave an enemy alive or un-captured to maybe kill more of his own friends, or himself, later. But who knows," I said, looking at their faces, not, for some reason, wanting to disappoint them. "Anything could happen in that war. It mostly did too. Did you ever see the documentary called

*Kontum Diary?* It's about an American soldier who brings such a captured diary back to the guy who'd owned it. There's also one, *Iron Triangle*—you know, Beau Bridges, which tries to bring in your side. Though mostly you're right—our films center on the American experience. As you'd expect. The thing is, the Americans I've seen in the Vietnamese films have mostly been terrible stereotypes also." I told them about a made-for-television movie I'd watched in my hotel room the night before in which the American G.I.'s were played by Vietnamese actors wearing blue contact lenses, making them look particularly demonic. "Though I guess turn-about is fair play," I said.

"Yes," Hanh said impatiently. She is small and slight and at that moment looked to be fifteen years old. A very determined and fierce fifteen-year-old. One who was going to get her way. "We really want to avoid stereotypes. We want a typical American."

"If you go with the attitude you want a typical American, then you're inevitably going to create a stereotypical American," I said, and sipped my tea. I was pleased with the phrase. It sounded mellifluous and wise, the kind of Yoda-dictum I'd pronounce to a creative-writing workshop. It seemed to impress both of them too. They nodded enthusiastically. "You're right, uncle," Hanh said, smiling sweetly, turning the ambush around. "So why don't you write that part for us?"

The script, Binh said, would be based on the war experiences of several real people, though their names would be changed, and their stories, as necessary, shaped to the needs of the narrative. The thread that would weave it together was the story of a combat cameraman, based on the famous documentary film-maker Tran Van Thuy, who was one of their advisors, and who would give them some of the film he had shot during the war. Another character, a poet named Van, was to be the character the American (his name, they insisted, would be the easily pronounceable "John") spared. The stories were to take place during the war, in 1968, and thirty years later, as the lives of the characters are seen again on the twenty-fifth anniversary of the fall of Saigon. The untold stories, kept from the children, as if not to stain them; the stored rage, liberated from locked boxes and closed, darkened rooms. Maybe, they suggested, I could even come and play the part of John as a middle-aged man. They liked the idea of using a real American veteran. Well, I said doubtfully. I wasn't an actor. Nor had I been a grunt. Binh laughed suddenly. "But you can be John, Wayne. Ha! John Wayne, yes?" Yes, I said, yes, I got it.

I agreed to look at the rest of the script and think about writing the American segment when I got back home, though I still had doubts. I didn't think the kids, as they had become in my mind, had much of a chance of getting this film made.

Neither, it turned out, did anybody else. In Vietnam, Binh and Hanh had been told constantly why they couldn't do it. They had taken out loans and eventually even rented their house out and moved in with Binh's parents. They couldn't do it on that amount of money, they were told. It was impossible to get all the permissions they needed for location shots. Not to mention the military equipment. Not to mention the actors. And no war film had been done as a joint production with a foreign company. They didn't have the money, the most up-to-date equipment, or the manpower. They couldn't do it. Everyone said they couldn't do it. Only they didn't know they couldn't do it. They couldn't imagine not doing it. So of course they were getting it done. It all seemed at once very familiar. A lesson lost on MacNamara, Johnson, and Nixon. One I should have known. They really were VC.

"Are you disappointed?" the girl in the baseball hat asks me.

I look at her, startled, as if she has tapped into my thoughts. "Excuse me?"

She seems embarrassed. "I'm sorry, *xin loi.* I mean about the extras."

"No. It'll be O.K...

Our plan that day had been to use Marines from the embassy to take the roles of American troops. A tentative agreement had been made, and the Marines seemed to get a kick out of the idea, but a Higher Up from the embassy nixed their participation, and we were stuck without American extras.

"It's not that bad," Fiona Reilly, the Australian production coordinator, had said earlier that morning. "A lot of the Marines are too bulked up—all that weight-lifting. They have different bodies than the pictures you see of men in the war." She touched her hair nervously. "Steve," she named the extras coordinator, "is rounding up some guys from the hostels and bars. Oh, and we lost the guy who was doing Young John."

"How are you, Fiona?"

"Harassed and harried, mate."

"Sure. And you're probably right about the Marines. But at least there'd be some African Americans. It wouldn't look right otherwise."

The pick-up squad of extras Steve had culled from the bars and hostels began showing up at about seven. None of them were black. None of them were American. They were

French, English, Spanish, and one Brazilian, Roberto, a film school student in Australia who had volunteered and was paying his own way to work on the movie. He was dying to play an American soldier. It was something he always wondered about, he told me, how it would feel for young men his age, to go through that ordeal. I had assigned him the heavy radio, thinking: if he wants to suffer.

We drive north, out of the flat rice-field country, up into dark, limestone mountains, pocked with caves and draped with mist. The site that will substitute for the southern battlefields is a small, uneven plateau: meadows, small paddies and corn fields, and scrub jungle cupped between the hills and peaks on all sides. It had been an area, in fact, where the Viet Minh had fought a number of battles with the French. The set people have built a small firebase: sandbag rimmed holes and emplacements, barbed wire, machine guns.

When we arrive at the site, the extras strip to their underpants, and I work with the two prop women to get them dressed, have them put on the helmets, flak jackets and cartridge belts dangling with canteens and entrenching tools. The prop women are looking at me uneasily. One has chains of some shiny metal dog-tags looped around her hand, dangling like rosaries. I ask her to find some black tape and wrap the tags before she gives them out to the extras. Why? she asks me. So they wouldn't be targets, I say ridiculously.

The woman wears a kerchief over her lower face, against the dust, and a conical hat. A number of times I turn to catch her staring at me. She appears to be middle-aged, though it is hard to tell. I help her stick various things under the boys' helmet bands, twigs, mosquito repellent bottles, packs of cigarettes. Roberto has a crumpled pack of Marlboro Lights. No, I tell him, those didn't exist then.

"He should use Salem," the woman says to me suddenly, in Vietnamese, her eyes meeting mine, shining with some inner amusement or malevolence. I stare at her. When I would go into the hamlets around our perimeter, the people always wanted that brand; Salems were like currency. I didn't find out until much later that they were Ho Chi Minh's favorite brand, and I'd always bring a pack or two for the family of a little girl I'd become attached to, whenever I went on patrol.

For a moment I have the fantasy the prop woman could be her—that radiant child that had become for me emblematic of the beauty destroyed by the war. Of course she couldn't be, but this woman had to have been in the South, among the American soldiers, to remember that brand, hadn't she? How does she remember us? She looks at me, the cloth still concealing her mouth, the things it might tell me. Then she retreats into the shadows in the back of the prop bus, taking her story with her. I don't chase it.

The extras pull on the worn boots, and I show them how to blouse their trousers. They are standing in a row, as if in formation. I stare at their boots, caked already with the red, laterite mud, and feel something freeze in me. It is one of those moments that has happened less and less frequently as I have returned to Vietnam, when I'd see or hear something that would spin me into the past. But the movie isn't helping.

*You can be John, Wayne. Ha! John Wayne, yes? Get it?*

*Out-take: Perimeter*

John's position is in a section of the perimeter that traverses the western slope of the Hill: a string of sandbagged holes, rigged with ponchos against the rain. Two men and an M-60 machine gun in each. At the base of the slope, rows of concertina wire separate the camp from the landscape: beyond it some scrub-jungle and a string of hamlets, the village of Truong Toan. His first night, sitting in the muddy hole, rain running down his neck under his poncho, peering out over the dripping barrel of the gun at the tangle of trees illuminated sporadically by flares fired off by a mortar team behind the hill, he finds he is sitting in his hole not only with the kid next to him, but with a picture of himself in his own mind. The cynical, wisecracking, put-upon yet enduring grunt. Helmeted, flak-jacketed, his boots and utilities already stiff with mud.

It is what he wanted. After infantry training at Camp Geiger, he'd been furious at being given a clerk's MOS, Military Occupational Specialty. John hadn't joined the Marines to go to war as a clerk. He had become a very bad one. Lost Service Record Books, turned in orders and reports rendered hieroglyphic with typos, smudged with tiger stripes of ink. *What the hell do you want?* Gunny Halloran, the S-1 chief had asked him, shaking his head, staring at John with ravaged eyes that were netted with the same skein of veins that crept up from his cratered nose, three rows of ribbons on his chest: bronze star, purple hearts, the Chosin Reservoir. *You want to get into it?* He waved in the vague direction of the war, a thousand miles south of the squadron office at Camp Schwab. *Do you know what you're asking for?* John, shocked, had seen tears well, spill from the corners of Halloran's eyes. He'd looked away. Outside the window, a dusty column of grunts from the Third Marines was passing by: Schwab was the jumping off point into a transformation he had deemed necessary for himself. Gunny, it don't feel right, that those guys, he said. You're a fucking idiot, Halloran replied. Get the hell out of my sight.

He had, all the way to here. When he'd gotten to Vietnam, convoyed out to a hill north of the Chu Lai base, just above the flats where the Ky Ha helicopter base would be built, he was assigned to help build the hootches that would gradually replace the tents of the initial settlement, and to perimeter security. Now he practices his thousand-yard stare. John as a character John has created. Towards three in the morning, the perimeter is put on full alert and, moments later, a few rounds of sniper fire tear into the hillside a hundred yards to his left. John returns fire. He feels no fear, only triumph. He's finally arrived. He's gotten the part.

It was like this. One night in the hole, one man trying to sleep on the two lined up sandbags that keep him, barely, out of the water in the bottom of the hole, the other man peering out at the night. Fifty percent alert. If they receive any fire, or an alert, they go to a hundred percent, and neither sleeps. Days they either work building tin-roofed hootches, or go on patrols in and around Truong Toan, sometimes security, sometimes MEDCAP—Medical Civic Action Patrols, taking the corpsmen out to run clinics in the village. Winning hearts and minds. The villagers smiling, nodding: one little girl attaching herself to John; he visits her family, eats rice with them. He's a Kennedy kid; he will go where the desire for freedom calls. He gives them Salems, the villagers crazy for the brand; they smile at him more, exotic, pitifully poor, grateful. It is early in the war. He is there to save them, to ask not what his country can do for him, to do it to them instead. The G.I. and the kids, chewing gum and cigarettes. He isn't sure why they desecrate the pictures of the prime minister that the Ruff Puffs, the local government militia, are sticking on the walls.

He watches with satisfaction as his jungle boots wear in, get scrapped, caked with red mud, sees in them a gauge of the experience that he, John, himself, is taking on.

Some nights he goes out, unauthorized, with patrols and ambushes from the experienced platoon of grunts from the Fourth Marines that are assigned to help beef up the perimeter, teach them things, after one of the boys John had been with on Okinawa loses his right foot to a rifle grenade fired from the tree line. The man assigned to John's hole is a slight, blond machine-gunner named Besar, who's been in country nine months.

Besar teaches John a number of things. He digs two new holes, each about fifty yards from their position, but leaves them unmarked by sandbags. The first time they receive fire, he makes John roll out behind the hole, carry the machine gun over to the new hole, fire from there. The next day, going out through the wire, he shows John the stick on the ground pointed towards their position, a marker placed by the VC. That afternoon, as they move through a rice field on the outskirts of Truong Toan, one of the villagers who has smiled and spoken to John during MEDCAPS walks casually by the patrol, a hoe over his shoulder. You souvenir me Salem? he asks John, and Besar wheels suddenly and cracks his jaw with his rifle butt. The man writhes on the ground, holding his jaw, his front teeth gone, as the squad walks silently past.

What the fuck did you do that for? John demands.

Besar ignores him. That evening, their backs against the sandbags, he takes a photo out of his breast pocket, passes it to John. It is from an ambush they'd done, down on the Batangan Pennisula, Besar says. He'd gotten the most body count out of it—picked up an R&R in Bangkok as a prize. The ten or twelve bodies in the Polaroid are heaped on top of each other, blood-laced flesh swollen out in what seemed huge lumps, as if from some strange plague. They are all women and children. There are shattered baskets on the ground around them, some still clutched by dead hands. Mangoes and green bananas spill from them. Somehow the baskets and the bodies seem of equal importance or weight.

Where the fuck do you think you are? Besar asks him.

The memory of the photo becomes a picture that develops in front of his eyes whenever he brings his attention to it, and sometimes when he doesn't. Blank white. Faint suggestions of shape and color. Stains. The shapes finding their forms, small oblongs, longer oblongs. This a child, that a woman. The colors blossoming, spreading. The details sharper, petaled flesh, glazed open eyes. Clarifying.

It was like this. Not long in country, sleeping for the first time on his mosquito-netted rack in camp, he's awakened by one of the S-1 clerks, excited: there has been a big operation, volunteers are being asked to help unload wounded from the helicopters. He goes down to the pad next to B-Med and is immediately pressed into service as a stretcher-bearer. It is raining. John stares at the gunner in the first helicopter. He doesn't know that in a few months he will be sitting behind a machine gun in another helicopter, watching volunteers pulling out human forms, as if by magic, from the wounded and dead piled near his feet like a heap of dirty clothes. The boys he helps from the hatches of the UH-34s now and forever change the way he defined the word 'wounded.' There are no clean movie wounds. Most often they are mangled. Hamburger limbs. Intestines spilling on the pad. A face with smoke steaming from eye sockets. A man with no jaw, his tongue dangling down and writhing like a muddy snake. Once, running back to the helicopters, he sees a thickset black man limping towards him, one arm in a muddy sling, one boot gone, foot shredded. I'm a corpsman, the man says to him or to someone not there. I'm a corpsman. He repeats the sentence in a monotone, over and over, John not sure if it represents defense or outrage at some vast injustice or an admission of helplessness. Looking into his face, John remembers practicing his thousand-yard stare. I'm a fucking idiot, he tells himself.

On his way back to the B-Med tent with another casualty, he sees two other things that he carries with him the rest of his life.

He sees Marines from the Ky Ha base camp crowding the wire around the helipad, all of them taking photographs of the dead and wounded.

He sees, lined up neatly just outside the tent, a row of the dead. They are all placed in the same position; that is, heads next to the tent, feet, when there were feet, out. There may be fifty of them. It is raining and their faces have all been covered with the same poncho he wears, and all of them are wearing his boots.

## ALTARS

Whenever I go to the Vietnam Veterans' Memorial in Washington, I always fear that the etched names on the wall, written on my reflection, will call up from my mind again that first time I saw the American dead: that line of Marines lying in the red mud outside the B-Med tent at Ky Ha— casualties, I found out years later, of an operation that had the pretty, high school prom-theme name of Harvest Moon. I always fear I'll see that line draining at the base of the wall, and sometimes I have. But it's been a long time since I had that moment of realization every soldier must have when he sees dead men wearing the so-familiar accoutrements of his own uniform and equipment, that recognition of his own mortality so alien to the mind of an 18 or 19 year old, and I don't want to see those reaped boys like that anymore, faceless and wearing my uniform. I'm not the one dead and I would like to honor them, for once, without the intrusion of my own thankfulness at surviving.

I don't know how well that will work out.

\*\*\*

On the bus, I mention to one of the other Vietnamese crew the feeling the movie had called to me of being caught in an endless loop of time. The boy nods—it reminded him, he says, of his uncle. Both his father and his uncle had fought in Quang Tri, and elsewhere. No, neither spoke of it. But his uncle had become like a wandering soul, he says, referring to the Vietnamese belief that the souls of people killed violently, far from home, will wander endlessly until an altar is built, until on a special day of the year, incense and offerings are left, and prayers said to bring them to peace. Until they are commemorated, their stories told. But his uncle's body hadn't died. Like many others, he had been in a unit where hundreds had gone south and only a handful returned. Now, still, always, he walked, continually, from north to south, tracing the journey he'd made in the war, haunting all the battlefields where he'd fought, Quang Tri to Tay Ninh. Visiting his friends, all of them dead. His endless march an altar to them, as was the story of it, told quietly in the back of the bus, seeping into my own stories, as was, perhaps, the movie itself—that flawed but inexorable need to grope towards memory and meaning. All of it coaxed out into the air by shame.

For the poet George Evans, the face of all the dead transfigure into one face, that of a childhood friend who preceded him into the war, warned him against the wastage of it, died as if to underscore that lesson.

*...monuments are taxidermy;*
*there is little retribution, little learning; what is lost*
*is forgotten; sometimes it gets so bad I'm not sure*
*I'm the one who lived...then come upon you in a field*
*—a one time soldier with a trick knee, flagging humor,*
*monsoon debt—and find you enfolded by fog as if by spirits,*
*and become the visage of all that's been*
*thrown from the world.*

At the Wall, our own altar to wandering spirits, I also seek out one name in particular, that of Lance Corporal James Childers, who died instead of me somewhere near Marble Mountain, Danang, in the year 1967.

The above is a dramatic statement, and a true one, but I don't want to make too much here of my own combat experience. I extended my tour six months for duty as a helicopter gunner out of both boredom and guilt, but the fly time for gunners, at least in the Marine Corps, was rotated and hence broken by long periods when we were not, as we said, on flight pay, and the war for me, as I suspect it was for many others, consisted of long stretches of boredom, sleeplessness, discomfort, mindless work, occasional hilarity, petty harassments, and small moral erosions, interspersed with moments of intense excitement and sometimes terror. Most of the latter, of course, took place when I was flying. The missions I remember the most vividly were the night medevacs: hanging over a machine gun, searching the Quang Tri blackness, waiting for the streams of green North Vietnamese tracers to come flying up towards the aircraft; when they did my own tracers flashing red, curving towards the ground: an image still so strong that it's ruined me for video games. The bottom would suddenly drop out of the world like a released trap door and we'd fall and land hard and they'd bring in the wounded and the dead while we'd feel the helicopter straining to lift off and be out of danger: we'd feel that in the tissues of our bodies. The wounded and the dead would lie on the deck around the gun mounts, and we'd get out of there. And when we landed the stretcher-bearers would carry out the hurt and unceremoniously drag out the dead and we'd wash the blood and other fluids off the deck with a hose and take off again to scoop up another load of names to be put on that black Wall near Constitution Avenue.

James Childers died in what was to have been the last week of the war for him. Our squadron was rotating to Okinawa to regroup and receive new aircraft, and he and I were in the small contingent left behind as a transition team.

It was the second time I had rotated to Okinawa: my other squadron had gone there and disbanded after a seven-month stint in Vietnam. The statistics of its tour there are perhaps telling of what it meant to be in a helicopter squadron in Vietnam in 1966-1967. According to a base newspaper clipping I still have, the squadron had flown over 25,000 hours during those seven months and participated in more than a dozen operations, including seven major pushes along the DMZ. The article mentions that the squadron averaged more than 200 medevacs a month, 25 per cent of them flown at night, and that seven aircraft were lost during this period. It tells how one helicopter was brought back to base with more than 500 bullet holes in it, and another with 800. These last facts don't seem accurate to me: the holes were probably caused by shrapnel, not bullets. But holes they were.

The article does not mention the devastation that a North Vietnamese Army 12.7 mm or quad-50 caliber machine gun can wreak on low-flying helicopters, nor does it tell of Helicopter Valley, that deadly area near the Rockpile scattered with the crushed grasshoppers of shot-down helicopters, nor of the aircraft and crewman lost when one of our missions flew into a barrage of American artillery on its way to an emergency landing zone.

After my other squadron had disbanded, I came back to finish out my tour. It was my last week, and I was down to the last three days, but I was still scheduled to fly. The transition and the war had left both our squadron and the replacement squadron short-handed and everybody had to do everything. Childers and I were often thrown together on details that week. We were friends, but not particularly close—what we would call military acquaintances.

The facts of his death are simple enough. I was scheduled to be on standby flight status that night, but for a reason I've never known, I was told to switch times with him: Childers was scheduled to fly the next day. That night, the aircraft he was assigned to was called out on an emergency resupply mission to a hill near Danang. The helicopter was on approach when it came under fire. A single bullet penetrated it and the body of James Stanley Bernard Childers, entering just below the bottom edge of his flak jacket. He died an hour later on an operating table in Charlie Med, across the road from the Marble Mountain base camp.

It was not an unusual way for a helicopter crewman to die, nor do I consider the way we happened to switch places particularly miraculous. Freaks of fate become mundane in a war. For the next two days I flew his missions and I was more terrified than I had ever been. But the flights were all milk runs and I survived.

I survived and he didn't, and it was because of this simplest of reasons that memorials are built in the first place, and that I wanted to stop the flow of this narrative and remember James Childers, a nineteen-year-old boy I didn't know too well, but who died in my place and in your name, one of 58,226 who did the same. *The visage of all that's been thrown from the world.*

In the Vietnamese film *Wait Until the Tenth Month Comes* by the great director Dang Nhat Minh, a soldier tells a young boy that the boy's father—the soldier's comrade—has been killed in battle.

The boy stares at him.

"Why are you still alive?" he asks.

## DANCING ON CHAOS

We stand looking at the battlefield set. The extras are assuming poses, fiddling with their weapons. A man runs around them, waving a long pole attached to a bamboo cup filled with lit pitch, draping them in foul black smoke. Binh is squinting at the hills, pointing out something to Hanh, who stands next to him, holding a megaphone. Jonathan waves at the smoke-man, yells: "More, more, lay it on-la!" He grins at me. "What do you think?"

"It seems chaotic."

He winks, grins broadly at Hanh. "Chaotic—is that it, Hanh-oi? Never mind. It's all fun." He throws back his head and laughs. He laughs quite a bit. Whenever he stood next to Binh, it was like seeing two opposing forces of the universe: Jonathan tall, wide-faced, generously-paunched, smiling broadly, Binh short, sharp-chinned, thin, serious. Prosperity and Deprivation.

"Look at that jungle, those mountains, that field," he cries suddenly, sweeping his hand through the air. "In Singapore all the trees are transplants. Artificial-la. Not even the beaches are real: they truck in the sand. You come visit me in Singapore, you'll feel right at home," he tells me. "Westerners always do-la. Like you came from one spotless, identical hotel to another. Some ways, that's good—it's clean, it's safe-la—you can walk down the street—it's organized. I like it! But sometimes I don't. Sometimes I need a little chaos."

He moves behind the camera, said something to Moad Jeffri Yosuf, the Malaysian cameraman. The scene is nearly

46

as confusing as a battlefield, people scattered everywhere, milling, sitting, lying down, screaming at each other, shooting, laughing hysterically, and through it all runs a small, grinning man weaving curtains of smoke. Jonathan spins around also, running here and there, arranging people and equipment like furniture in a room, putting the actors and the camera where he wants them. He needs the chaos. He needs Hanoi or Saigon or Bangkok—not Singapore. Not everything explained. Not everything flowing at exactly the speed limit, everybody stopping just before the traffic light turned, nobody jaywalking, the filthy and insane forbidden to break into unexpected dances outside your air-conditioned window. He needs to have things falling apart so he can see how they should go together. He needs to touch the contradictory complexity which is the breath of truth. Looking at him now, framing shots with his hands, positioning people, the slight tremble under his controlled movements, his face, intent and hungry, I can feel something shift in me towards him and I understand, as if I can see it through my own eyes, how he is looking at the seethe around him, the frantic comings and goings and flowing: how all of it is being fitted to a design only he can see at this instant, that he will move towards inexorably, ruthlessly.

They wanted to get it right, Binh and Hanh had said. To open the stories gagged tightly in the mouth into the resonant testimony of art. O.K, I had thought when they told me what they had in mind about the character, I could do John as a poet, like Van, someone who would take the diary and then begin writing his own poetry in it, feeling a compulsion to continue the life of the Vietnamese soldier he'd spared, to become him. They would meet, John would give Van back his poetry, now continued into John's own. Their words and faces bringing each to life for the other. I'd had enough conversations with Vietnamese writers to imagine the meeting he and Van could have: two men who once could have killed each other suddenly seeing each other's human face. He would be, I thought, an easy character to write. I knew how John would feel, what he'd say. He was me, but not me. Not me, but me. He was my own out-take. It was always like that, writing a character, but it would be more so with John. *John Wayne. John but not Wayne. Get it?* I'd come back to Vietnam, as he would come back, looked into the eyes of the enemy as if into mirrors. Van was the man John didn't kill. He would instead take his diary. But why wouldn't he shoot or capture Van? In reality, I would have shot him, rather than let him live to kill more Americans; that is, me. It would be mawkish and sentimental, false, to have it happen in a moment of compassion for a fallen enemy. No, he'd take it because he somehow sensed that taking it *was* taking Van's life. He was stealing his enemy's soul. It was an act of pure hatred, that would turn into a curse, and then a blessing. He would take the diary home. He would have it translated, read Van's poetry, connect to it. He would begin writing in it, take off where Van stopped. But he'd write poetry. He'd take on Van's life, as if Van's soul had been translated to America, merged with his. It was the only way he, John, could express the experience. It had happened to many American veterans. The poetry that came from the war is some of the best American poetry ever written, and it has come from people who, in other circumstances would probably have never become poets: the sons of Pittsburgh ice-men, Ohio steel workers, Bogalusa share-croppers. When they came back from the most significant experience of their lives, they found they no longer spoke in the same language as the country that had sent them to it. Their minds and souls no longer saw the world in the same way, thought in the same terms, had the same references and loyalties. They had been born in Vietnam as much as they had been born in Pennsylvania or Louisiana. They had to create their own language to express what they knew. They had to suck it in and give it back so that it would seep into and change the people around them. They had to dance on chaos. They had to become poets. Or writers of fiction. Fiction had seemed to me the only way to express it when I'd came back from Vietnam, when I sat for weeks on end in a concrete box on Ventura Boulevard, watching the war in silent black and white on a ten-inch television sitting like an eye on a beige pressed-wood dresser. Days I took classes and worked a job the State of California employment office had gotten for me at the warehouse of a porno publisher. I'd stand alone in a cavernous warehouse in Van Nuys, pulling covers decorated with pictures of splayed women off magazines returned from adult book stores, so that the publisher could resell them. Shelved all around me were boxes of paperbacks: *The Sexual Habits of College Coeds, Secrets of the SS Brothels, Backdoor Delights, Oriental Delights.* The books were written, for the most part, by housewives and retirees from the Valley. They used academic titles and the names of local streets for their pen names. Dr. Sherman Way, PhD. I prepared and shipped the boxes to adult book stores across the nation. But most of my work was with the magazines. Their titles were more direct and seemed to bring the terminology of the war I'd just come back to into the warehouse with me: *Slanty Sluts, Anal Asians, Oriental Orifices*—always, it seems, that turn back to the East. The magazines were printed without dates. Unsold copies were remaindered by the stores, and returned for credit. I was the manual stripper (MS on the company's orientation sheet). I would pick up a carton of *Slanty Sluts* from the floor and put it on a long table, take out one *Slut*, pull the front and rear cover to one side with my left hand, hold down the body of the magazine with the palm of my right and the weight of my body, and neatly pull off the cover. Bing-bang, the past was gone. That easy. I'd put the stripped magazine (SM) into another box. When the boxes were full, they were taken away by a silent Mormon dwarf who drove a very small forklift. I never knew if the forklift had been built especially for the man or how the new covers were put on. I didn't care. I saw the covers twice: once when I first took the returned magazine (RM) from its box, and then in the growing pile of discards on the floor next to me. The unifying aesthetic theme of the cover art seemed to be spreading. Vulnerability.

*John stood at his table, stripping covers. The girls looked at him, their eyes pleading. They were white, black, but very often Asian. He felt caught in another inevitable progression: the row of corpses he had seen at Ky Ha, the torn bodies packed inside the helicopter, the meat piled knee deep around him, the splayed, naked bodies of the women he processed. All of it was sex gone bad. He put his sweated palm against their faces, their breasts, their pink and pearly genitals, and pushed, separated them. They screamed. They moaned. They piled around his legs, clung to his knees, pulled at him, grabbed the belt of his machine gun as it whipped through the air. Hot casings showered them. They looked like flesh turned into pudding. How had he gotten here? He felt like a bullet on a linked belt, part of an inevitable but senseless progression from the communal to the isolate. He had been subsumed, connected, and now torn apart. Linked by fear and sleeplessness to the other boy in his foxhole, their days and nights and dreams melting into each other, tied to the other holes by flares and stories, born sliding through the opening between coils of barbed wire, a green creature bristling with weapons, umbilical corded by the intercom in his helmet and the gunner's belt clipped to his waist to the other crew in the belly of the helicopter, lying on a sandy cot, one of a row of sandy cots under the tin roof of a hootch at Marble Mountain, his breaths and groans and farts contributing, creating the air they all breathed; packed into a concrete barracks on Okinawa, all of them sitting on their racks, staring, somewhat bewildered; the same look they wore on their faces on the C-131 which took them across the Pacific, spewed them out in San Francisco, scattered them* until I woke up one dazed morning to find myself utterly alone in a ten-by-twelve studio apartment in a small complex of white and blue concrete boxes between two gas stations on Ventura Boulevard in Van Nuys. It held a stained, linty, purple rug, a monk's bed, a black velvet Keene picture, a chipped desk and bureau, and a black and white TV. Shadows from my war played on it, grainy, illusionary. How had I gotten here? What the fuck had all that been about? Where was everybody? I developed the film I'd taken in Vietnam, spent hours and then sleepless nights arranging and rearranging an album of photographs. As if to reassure myself that it had been real, as if to prove the existence of my own past, as streams of traffic passed indifferently outside my window, people on their way to their lives, separated yet intertwined with a parade of the dead and forgotten, like the Bangkok crowds of busy Thais and old Western men, transparent as ghosts. As if I were an out-take from whatever movie was going on. I wanted to stick my head out and scream at them. Instead I wrote stories. Created a character like John, in order to be John and Not-John and so more than both. Remembered incidents that seemed, maybe, to stand for the whole thing, and tore them apart and re-pasted them, retold them, moment by moment, until they did.

REVISION


Jonathan and Binh want the "Americans" to chase Van through some scrub-brush, perhaps a square acre of field framed by exquisitely lovely country, the jagged limestone mountains standing around us like a ring of carved, ancient bones, their fissures and cracks furred with verdigris. Around the field, at the base of the mountains and jungled hills, are lush rice fields, a patrol of massive water buffalo moving on their periphery. Binh has arranged marks for the extras to follow, scraps of white paper pinned to the ground.

I'd written some lines between Van and the American: Van asking how his new friend saw the country. "I can't see anything for what it is," the American replies. "Everything contains itself and the past. But sometimes, now, with you, I just see the beauty of the place. It's as if the war is gone." In this place, with these kids running through it with equipment and rifles and helmets, only the first part of that statement seems true to me. The heat and the landscape are putting me back on the perimeter, into that hyper-edginess in which everything moves a few frames more slowly, larger than life, the colors brighter, the clarity so sharp it cuts, sounds and sights slapping into the brain. But it is as if I am experiencing everything through a series of lenses whose edges overlap and blur what they frame into each other: my memories of the real war, a sensory memory of walking through some scrub jungle on patrol near Ky Ha, the vivid landscape here peopled by these G.I.s, and Vietnamese in front of my eyes now, the memories of films I've seen, the images my own mind stirred into being from my reading, from my writing. It's a country I've been in before when I'm trying to write a book and the characters begin becoming real and I feel myself becoming a character in their story; it's the way—and here the circle loops around, touches its ends together—I felt in the war itself.

The extras had been soaked with sweat by the time we'd gotten them in jungle utilities, gear, helmets and flak jackets, and after one five-minute chase they pant so hard they seem to be hyperventilating. Wasted. In the summer heat the grunts often wouldn't wear flak jackets. But they would hump ten, twenty kilometers a day, over hills like the one looming over us, tangled with vines and bamboo. I line up my men, thinking of them that way, *my men*, seeing my little fire team through the eyes of a twenty-year-old Marine sergeant. I tell them to drink more water. I make them blouse their trousers. Michael, the boy who is playing the part of my character as a young soldier, seems uncomfortable with his rifle. He pushes its barrel and flash suppressor down into the dirt, screwing the rifle into the ground. It puts whatever is left of the sergeant in me on edge: I want to snatch the piece away from him, scream at him. Finally, I reach down, cradle my hand under the barrel and push it out of the dirt, and then take the rifle from him, as if I want to examine it. Its metal is worn to silver and its plastic casing cracked. The breech is stamped "Property of the United States Government." I give it back to him. He has been chosen for the part as a last-minute replacement because he has my color eyes and height. "I hate guns," he says. "I hate the whole idea of war and killing," he says, and buries the barrel in the dirt again. I stare at him, at what he is doing, as if at a younger self, trying frantically across the shimmer of heat and time to tell me something that he's learned.

When the first takes are finished, the extras collapse in the dirt.

We are supposed to be doing this scene in Quang Tri

province but we hadn't gone, finally, because the war was literally still there: too much unexploded ordnance hidden in the ground, and some barrels the army had found that were leaking what they suspected was dioxin into the nearby river. In July of 1966, the North Vietnamese 324B Division, some 10,500 of the best soldiers the People's Army had, had come down into that province over the Demilitarized Zone. It was a month when I was, as we said, on flight pay. Our squadron was part of the force of Marines—an air group and six infantry battalions—sent north to meet the 324B. These were not the VC guerillas the Marines had gotten used to fighting around Danang and Chu Lai: they were People's Army of Vietnam, North Vietnamese regulars—uniformed, pith-helmeted and well-armed, including anti-aircraft weaponry—20 millimeter cannon, and four-barreled fifty caliber machine guns. On the first day of the operation, our squadron, and one other, lost five helicopters between us. The 324B was stopped after a two month battle in the hills and jungle around the DMZ. But that's a statement for a history book, and for my own part of it what is left are only fragmented images of landing in terrifying darkness, split by flashes of green tracers, loading the helicopter with dead and broken Marines all wearing the uniforms and equipment and boots of the boys taking a break now in this clearing, lying around me in a star of bodies in the red dirt.

We are called back over to do the shoot again. The boys rise. Action, the director screams, and they run after Van, and then are called back and do it again. As the light fades, so do their faces, until they become glowing blurs under the helmets, above the flak jackets, the flapping, stained jungle utilities whose origin I didn't want to think about, the rifles taken from God-knew-whose hands, until I see only some frantic, possessed dance, that ragged clothing wrapped around whatever had been trapped in it, running forever, called back again and again to follow the pattern of marks laid on this ground.

Late in the afternoon, the light in danger of fading, we finally shoot the scene where John takes Van's diary. Van lies on the ground, stunned and bleeding. John comes cautiously out of the brush, his rifle trained on Van's head. On the ground, a few feet ahead of the supine soldier, is a battered yellow and red book; the same book in which we have seen Van writing his poetry. With one hand holding his rifle, pointing its clogged barrel steadily at Van's head, John squats, touches the diary. He will take it, write in it. His words and Van's will intertwine, connect. He will take on Van's life, as if Van's soul had been translated to America, merged with his. Or as if his soul had remained here.

He rises slowly, his eyes locked with Van's, giving himself a chance to give Van the chance that I would never have given him.

# SCENE THREE
## Fast Forward:
## 2004

# MISSING IN ACTION

I'd never revisited Quang Tri, or any of the areas where I'd been during the war until four years after doing *Stork*, going then, as it were, for another film: a documentary being shot by a group of New York University film students about their generation's view of the war. Several of the students had fathers in the war—my own son, though not in the course, also joined us in the middle of the trip—and three of those were Viet Kieu, overseas Vietnamese whose fathers had been in the South Vietnamese Army. Their teacher, and the originator of the course, was an Israeli film director named Judd Ne'eman. Judd had been a combat surgeon in a paratroop brigade during Israel's wars, and was active in that country's peace movement. He was interested in the films of the Vietnam war and in the reconciliation through literature work I and my friends had done with the Vietnamese, as if it could be a model for a postwar process in the Middle East. A hope that seemed more and more remote every day of that year.

I had been back to Vietnam many times by then, including my work on *Song of the Stork,* and I didn't expect to be very affected by any geographical pilgrimage: such a journey, the veteran revisiting old battlefields, had become a cliché and a staple of the tourist industry. In any case, I didn't feel my own experiences were traumatic or dramatic enough to evoke the wracked grief I'd seen in other veterans who'd returned to the killing fields. Yet three weeks before the trip, my body went into rebellion: my back, without any excuse or warning, going into massive spasms that left it impossible for me to sit without hot wires of agony shooting into my hips and back, a condition that has settled finally and chronically into knots of pain that serve as permanent reminders. Then, a week before I was to leave, my heart went into a wild arterial defibrillation that landed me in the hospital and made my wife demand that I give up the trip.

But I'd made too much of a commitment to the project by then, and I stocked up on Cardizem and oxycodene and aspirin and got on a plane. We spent time in Hanoi, interviewing the Vietnamese writers I knew there, and then went to central Vietnam, the area that we called I Corps during the war. We were accompanied by Tran Van Thuy, the film-maker who had been the basis for the character Vinh, the NVA cameraman, in *Song of the Stork*: he and I had become friends by then, though at the time of the last scene I described shooting in that film, we hadn't yet met.

We were in the Hanoi Documentary Film Studio, watching a converted tape of the black and white combat footage Thuy had shot in Quang Tri and Quang Nam when I came to realize that, just like all my other trips to Vietnam, this one would also resonate with situations that rightly belonged to the charged serendipity of fiction. Thuy's shadowed face was strobed with flickers of light from the small television screen, looking as it had during the opening scene of *Stork*. He had, from the beginning, taken his role as a recorder of history seriously, a feeling underscored for him by the fact all the other cameramen in his unit had died. Looking at the footage, it was unclear how he hadn't. Some of the film was standard stuff—happy villagers supporting the NLF—but much of it was scenes of actual combat, including scenes of American aircraft bombing and strafing yards from where he must have been, and even a sequence of going with a Viet Cong squad to blow up a bridge. There was a striking image of a beautiful VC girl guerilla, who turned her face suddenly to reveal the other side of it caved and carved by bullets. It was all shot at the time and in the places

I'd been in the war. Yet my emotions watching the film were somewhat secondhand: the absence of a sound track, the buzz of neon lighting elsewhere in the studio, the film's grainy, black and white quality, made it distant, as historical as Brady photographs of the Civil War—that is, until one image snagged my eye and I felt an icy hand squeezing my heart. "Shit," I said. "Stop the film. Rewind it. Can you rewind?" The image had been of some helicopter wreckage, and when the tape was slowly rewound, frozen, I saw that I had seem what I thought I'd seen: the call sign visible on the wreck was YT, Yankee Tango: this was a helicopter from my squadron, Marine Medium Helicopter Squadron 164. It was as if I had seen a corpse with a familiar, no, a known face, in a photograph of the dead at Antietam. I asked Thuy for details, but he could remember little—only that this had probably been in Quang Tri, and he hadn't seen the helicopter go down, only filmed the wreckage.

A week later, we were on a bus on Route 9, the road that ran parallel to the old DMZ, from Dong Ha to Khe Sanh, looking at the mountains where that helicopter had probably crashed, staring at the jungled peaks where the Marines had fought the 324B in 1966 during the operation in which I'd flown. Yet there was a Disney-ride quality to it: the mountains framed and contained by the safety of windows; Cutter's Ridge, the Rockpile, where our helicopters would land on a dime to resupply the observation post there, both flat against the sky, like exhibits of themselves...or like the diorama of the battle of Dien Bien Phu we had seen in the Military Museum in Hanoi with benches in front of it for the schoolkids brought in for history lessons.

In fact, Mr. Truc, our affable official "host" from the Ministry of Culture, wanted to compare Khe Sanh to Dien Bien Phu: a version of history reinforced by the carved bas-relief at the entrance to the small Khe Sanh museum, which shows panicky little Americans being overrun and surrendering to the People's Army. It was, I thought—and said to the students when I asked Truc to relinquish the microphone—both inaccurate and somewhat ironic for him to make that comparison, since it was the one that General Giap, the commander of the People's Army, had wanted the American high command to believe, thus tying up 5,000 Marines to defend the Khe Sanh plateau while meanwhile he threw his forces against the major cities, overrunning them; the Viet Cong penetrating even to the heart of Saigon. The Tet offensive did, as Mr. Truc said, mark a turning point in the war, caused the loss of confidence of the American public and Congress—but unlike the French at Dien Bien Phu, I said, growing somewhat heated, the Khe Sanh combat base was never overrun, never surrendered, even though the Marines had been surrounded and pounded by some 40,000 North Vietnamese soldiers.

Truc grinned at me, and I switched off the mike. I was surprised at my reaction. At my anger. I liked Truc and I hadn't been at Khe Sanh during the siege, though I had flown into it on missions during 1966 when it was being built up, including one nearby to rescue a downed army plane. But it had been the way truth was twisted to fit the needs of power or of the moment that had gotten us into the war in the first place, and, looking at the faces of the students on the bus, seeing my son's face, backdropped by those mountains from which I'd helped pull the bodies of others their, and his, age, I thought, not for the first time on this trip, about the more recent convenient and selective reshapings of history made by men who had never seen those bodies packed into the helicopters; who had kept their own bodies safe at home—missing from action—and waved the flag they stood in front of now as they sent other kids, also the age of these kids on the bus, to be torn apart on the streets of Baghdad and Fallujah. I was suddenly filled with anger, an old rage, the stored rage, that had never left me, that still lived somewhere in me, that twisted the muscles and bones of my body and raced and skipped my heart, and that it had been generated by Mr. Truc's own official version of reconfigured history made no difference at all.

The last time I'd landed at Khe Sanh the Marine presence was just being built up, and it was still mostly a small Special Forces base that was attempting to intersect the Ho Chi Minh Trail, not far from where my future friend Le Minh Khue, then a girl of 16, was working to keep that Trail open. It was in fact beautiful to fly over those deadly mountains, with their jungled vistas oddly Adirondack-like in places, waterfalls curving silver over white rocks below us, sometimes their misted spray creating dancing rainbows under the helicopter. The area around our LZ was, and still is, inhabited by Bru mountain people, and I remember sitting outside the helicopter when a loin-clothed Bru youth came up, toting a crossbow, to bum a cigarette. I teased him, patting the barrel of my .50 caliber machine gun, sticking out of the port over our heads, and then pointing at the bow. He grinned, spun around and shot the sliver of a bolt into some daisy speckled grass about fifteen yards away. Big deal, I thought, and then he retrieved the bolt and showed me how he had skewered a grasshopper, mouth to ass, that I hadn't even seen.

The cleared area at Khe Sanh today is not much bigger than that LZ: there are a few new looking sandbag bunkers erected to suggest the old Marine positions, a small museum, a completely intact and very clean U.S. Army Chinook helicopter near a small pile of wreckage: a tossed salad of helicopter parts, rotors, and a tail assembly. Around it, the hills in which 40,000 North Vietnamese had surrounded the base, and which had been hit with more bomb tonnage than was used during all of World War Two, were verdant again in the sunlight. To the east I could make out the peaks of Hills 881 North and South, where, a year before the siege, hundreds of Marines and NVA had fought with artillery and then with small arms and hand to hand, and where, after the battle, dead Marines were found lying next to their stripped down M-16s, shot in the head—the weapons, newly issued to them, failing to stand up to the conditions of jungle and battle.

Looking at those hills, lush and peaceful in the sunlight, Brian, one of the NYU students, remarked that it was impossible to imagine that once people had killed one another on them. But the hill battles, from the 30th of April 1967 to the 5th of May, though eclipsed by the famous siege, were as fierce as any in the history of American—and Vietnamese—warfare. At the time, unable to spot the North Vietnamese positions, and expecting to find only a small unit defending the hill, the Marines ascending it ran into instead a well dug-in and fortified North Vietnamese battalion. The subsequent combat was so intense that at one point the Marines, in spite of the maxim put into every Marine's head from boot camp on, had to abandon the bodies of 37 of their comrades on top of the hill.

A Navy chaplain at Khe Sanh, Ray Stubbe, wrote a description of the battle filled with scenes that could have come from an account of D-Day or Iwo Jima; they are sprinkled with the phrases "refused to leave," "refused to be evacuated," "completely disregarded his own safety." "LCpl Gary Eugene Mettler…ignored the heavy volume of enemy fire and moved his [machine gun] to a vantage point which provided optimal fire support for his platoon. While moving across the fireswept terrain, he was painfully wounded. He refused medical evacuation and succeeded in placing his weapon and delivering accurate suppressive fire against the hostile positions." "Although 2Lt Bruce Edwin Griesmer…was seriously wounded in the initial burst of fire, he continued to command the situation…continually refusing medical evacuation…until overcome with pain and loss of blood, he lost consciousness." "One of the Navy Corpsmen, HN Richard L. Kinney, rushed forward through the intense enemy crossfire, moving from one injured Marine to another to attend to their wounds. While thus serving his fellowmen, he was killed by the enemy." "Hospitalman John Charles Burke, Jr., completely disregarded his own safety as he dashed through the heavy volume of fire to aid the fallen Marines....he fearlessly lay in a prone position shielding a man while he gave him medical aid, undoubtedly saving the man's life." "SSgt Santos, unconcerned for his own life, went from bunker to bunker, spraying the area with rounds and throwing grenades. At one point he caught a live grenade and dropped it into an enemy bunker, saving many Marines' lives." "Realizing the necessity of, supplying the advance squad with ammunition, PFC Dorsey Burwin Williams unhesitatingly exposed himself to enemy fire by crawling forward with ammunition...Williams received a painful shoulder wound, but refused to return to safety... Approximately ten meters from the advance squad, PFC Williams threw several magazines of ammunition to them, while at the same time enemy soldiers rushed from the thick foliage. Reacting quickly, PFC Williams wounded the enemy soldiers, but before he could again fire, the enemy soldier fired a burst of automatic weapons fire into his head, killing him."

It was the language of medal citations, and reading Stubbe's descriptions I thought how inadequate phrases such as "exposed himself to enemy fire" were to describe someone willing to move at all in the eardrum-cracking din of a fire fight, as projectiles he has seen split and mutilate the flesh of his companions scribble the air around him. I remembered a crew chief describing how he had seen a squad of infantry he'd just landed move, inexorably, in the leap frog game called fire-team rushes towards an enemy bunker, as one after another Marine went down, no one hesitating, falling like mown grass, and the crew chief, red with an anger he didn't know what to do with, the veins on his neck standing out, said, "I'd better never hear anyone put down the grunts. Not in my hearing." They fought sometimes with great cynicism, taking hills that they knew they'd give back, fighting with cut-rate, bargain basement weapons that got them killed, shot at and shit at and hit both ways; sometimes feeling—after a thunder storm prevented them from getting air support and then hit them with a lightning bolt that took out three Marines as well—that even God was against them, and yet fighting always with great courage, as did the boys who defended those hills, as did the boys who defended the base whose remains we were on now, and part of the rage I felt came from that, from the waste of those who could and did give so much, from any history that would make them less; any history that would use their courage to waste other generations. They all deserved better than that mural which, in denigrating an enemy, denigrated the courage of both sides, and they had all deserved wiser elders than the old men who had brought them there and then stood back and cheered them on while they died on those fire-swept slopes.

As I looked at the hills, three figures came walking down the dirt road towards us, clarifying into three middle-aged Vietnamese men, one of whom, tall for a Vietnamese, was wearing an old NVA olive cap. The man in the middle, Truc told us, translating Tran Van Thuy's questions, was in charge of a team that searched this area for missing remains. There are still 300,000 Vietnamese missing, and finding and identifying them is a continuing mission, as it is for the Americans. He had found what he believed were the remains of soldiers who had been in the two units of the other men: they would help him make the identification, then bring back what there was for burial. One of the men had been in a reconnaissance platoon during the Khe Sanh battle. I asked him how close he had come to the American positions, and he said, "through the wire." How was that possible? I asked, and to my surprise he showed us, getting down in the grass sprinkled with the same daisies I remembered and doing the Vietnamese low crawl: stop, wait, flow like a shadow.

The other, the tall man, had been a 12.7mm anti-aircraft gunner: a weapon used against our helicopters in this area.

It was another face emerging out of the jungle for me, though the deadly connection I might have had with this man was more direct than any of the other veterans of the other side I'd met. Then we could have shot at each other, he said, when he was told what I had been, and he smiled grimly and we shook hands, though there was a wary, respectful coolness on both our parts that was unlike the experience I'd had with other veterans. I wasn't unhappy about that—sometimes it seemed too easy, a mutual forgiving that edged into premature forgetfulness, and this man was coming now to reclaim the bodies of friends we had killed, and I had my own ghosts in these mountains.

Have you ever seen or heard ghosts? I asked the MIA team head. Of course, he said, and told of a disembodied voice directing him towards a place where he found the remains of a lost soldier. And American remains? I asked, and he said, yes, sometimes, and these were given to the American team operating in country. I glanced over at the three overseas Vietnamese students with us and then asked—thinking of inconvenient history—the same question about the remains of South Vietnamese army troops. We find them also sometimes, he said, and then, apologetically, to the question I would have asked next, we don't have the budget to do anything about them. They are just left where they are, he said, and I thought of the Vietnamese belief that until the souls of those killed violently and away from home are brought to peace through offerings and recognition, they will continue to angrily wander the earth.

I stole another look at the three Vietnamese-American students in the group. They had been trying hard not to differentiate themselves from the rest of the students. "I'm not going to be your token Viet Kieu subject," Jonathan

Nguyen said. But of course it was as futile for them to try to see this experience through the eyes of someone with no connection to Vietnam as it would have been for me, and I wanted them to be in the film, and was thinking of what their reaction would be when I'd asked my question about the dead.

I also didn't know how their parents felt about them coming on this trip. In the part of Southern California where Jonathan lived, there had been riots the year before when a book store owner had put a picture of Ho Chi Minh in the window. Anything to do with communist Vietnam was anathema. Although there has been a shift, and the majority of American tourists who came to Vietnam now were Vietnamese-American, there were still many in that community who refused to set foot in Vietnam, or to allow any person, or object from Vietnam to come to the United States: two years before there had been riots also when an exhibit of Vietnamese artists had been scheduled at the Los Angeles art museum. In 1995, I'd co-edited an anthology of postwar fiction from the United States and Vietnam with Le Minh Khue, the North Vietnamese youth brigade veteran, and Truong Hong Son, an ex-South Vietnamese officer who had fled Vietnam as a boat person to avoid being put in a re-education camp after the war, and has since become a NASA scientist and a leading literary scholar. His wife, left behind, had been imprisoned for a time when she had tried to join him. Yet Son was a leader in the move for reconciliation. When we brought Khue, and the Hanoi novelist Ho Anh Thai, to the States for a book tour, there had been emotional demonstrations against their presence mounted by Vietnamese-Americans in Seattle, San Francisco, and New Orleans. "We strongly oppose the presence of communist literary lackeys like Le Minh Khue and Ho Anh Thai," proclaimed a flyer issued by the "Organizations of the Vietnamese Community of Washington State (Re: Propaganda Ploys of Communist Vietnam)." "They're lazy," Son had said to me, bitterly, speaking about the people who had instigated the demonstrations. "They want to hang onto the past because they're lazy. They may work hard at everything else, but it's easier for them to never change."

Yet Son was equally outspoken about what he saw as the attitude of the Vietnamese government towards the overseas Vietnamese. There had been a sea change and the government was now welcoming Viet Kieu back, even—this year of 2004—Nguyen Cao Ky, the ex-prime minister, but when I had suggested Son accompany us on this trip, I was told quietly but firmly—not only by people in Vietnam, but also by Son himself—that while he would have no problems traveling around, his inclusion might very well make getting permission to do the film impossible. Nguyen Cao Ky had come as a businessman with a million dollars to invest, but Son had been publicly critical of some policies— including the policy towards the fallen dead of the other side. It was another reason I had asked my question to the head of the MIA team. When a Vietnamese government official had asked Son and other leading overseas Vietnamese to explore ways the overseas community could use their talents and money to help Vietnam, the Viet Kieu luminaries had suggested that there be two basic gestures of reconciliation on the government's part: legal distribution of overseas Vietnamese literary publications in Vietnam, and permission for relatives to visit the closed cemeteries for South Vietnamese soldiers, in order to burn incense at their graves.

It would happen someday, the official had replied regretfully, and when Son told me of the incident, I reminded him of the monument to the Confederate dead that stands some seven miles from my house in Southern Maryland, at the site of a former Federal prisoner of war camp. Over 3,000 prisoners had died there, but it was only in the 1930s that the government permitted the erection of a memorial to former enemies, even though they were countrymen. "Well, things should mover faster now," Son said dryly.

But the animosity between the Vietnamese from both

sides of the war—at least on the part of the generation that had fought the war—was deeper than any anger towards Americans. Family quarrels are always deeper and more bitter than any others, and the war had, like our own Civil War, divided the nation at the level of family, with brothers and sisters often fighting on different sides. In Saigon, as most of the people there still called Ho Chi Minh City, the NYU group would visit the actress-writer Nguyen Thi Minh Ngoc, whose mother had been Viet Cong and whose father had been a Southern government official. Hers wasn't an unusual case.

The three Viet Kieu students remained silent. Sometime later, when Jonathan did mention something, it was about my ghost question. "Any Vietnamese would understand that question," he said to some of the other students. "It's something—ghosts—my family would take for granted."

I was a little, egotistically, (you see, I'm sensitive to your concerns) disappointed that he hadn't commented on the question about what would happen to the remains of South Vietnamese soldiers, a question I'd asked hoping to draw him and the other Viet Kieu students in. But then I realized that he had.

# HUE

We'd spent the day before we came to Khe Sanh in Hue, hosted by Vo Que, a poet who had been a student in the Buddhist anti-war movement during the time of the fighting. The Buddhist peace movement in the South was one of the groups placed into a governing coalition by the NLF after they took Hue. Vo Que took us along the bullet-pocked walls of the Citadel, and then finally to a grouping of old American APC's and tanks, metal dinosaurs stuck in the midst of a weedy field. Nearby, children flew colorful kites. The signs, in Vietnamese and English, described the vehicles as being used by the Americans and sometimes by their Saigon puppet troops.

Thuy, Vo Que, and I stood next to the machines, three other dinosaurs, and spoke our own old stories. The student assigned to interview was Pauline Nguyen, another of the Viet Kieu. In the middle of the conversation, I glanced at her and saw her cheeks were wet with tears. She caught my glance and burst into tears, her shoulders heaving.

"Pauline?" I said, but Thuy moved to her, put an arm around her shoulder. She rested her head against it.

"It's just," she said. "I look at these machines, and my dad might have been in one of them. He'll never talk about it. But I came here to find Vietnam, to find him." She pointed at the sign, at the word "puppet." "But it's as if he's been erased."

Thuy patted her shoulder; he was used to dealing with the issue, sensitive to the language still used in the country,

But the poet, looked startled. And then thoughtful. As if

he'd suddenly seen the words he used and saw and heard every day through the eyes and ears of another. At least, that was my hope.

"As if he's been erased," Pauline said again.

This was the second time in my life that I had been in Hue.

By late 1966, I had been assigned to a helicopter squadron that was stationed off the edge of the Phu Bai airstrip, in a small area protected by a company of tanks, wagon-train circled, their guns pointing at the country. Occasionally, and more casually, protected by me as well, walking guard with a shotgun. It was the only weapon I pointed anywhere while I was in that unit, which was in the last stage of its tour. It would soon rotate to Okinawa to be disbanded (although I would be sent back to Vietnam), and my own rotation to flight duty never came up. That didn't bother me. A friend of mine from Ky Ha who had followed my example and also extended his tour for gunner duty went on his first mission and watched as the helicopter in front of him was hit by friendly fire, an artillery barrage someone forgot to call off in time. He came back gray-faced and ruined, told me how he had seen the shell seem to drift into the cargo hatch of the UH-34D before it exploded. The remains of the crew had to be identified by their dental patterns. I was sick of the war by then, though not because of that incident, which at the time I reacted to with a resigned numbness. Oh. We shot down our own crew. How 'bout that? It was a lethargy, a feeling of being suddenly very old, that may have come as a letdown after the adrenaline intensity of flying, or maybe from the curse of a tuning-fork nature, some bar inside me that took in, vibrated to everything happening around me, in two words: the war. What Michael Herr describes in *Dispatches* as an "informational Death of a Thousand Cuts, each cut so precise and subtle you don't even feel them accumulating, you just get up one morning and your ass falls off."

Mine had. The blankness that I felt erasing me in pieces, like a figure being erased by his animator in the Saturday morning cartoon shows I'd watch as a kid, was not manifested in any questioning of the war, but rather in a sense of detachment allowed by the sudden and relative safety of the place where I found myself. In the rear with the gear. Sometimes it was as if I were watching the world, myself, through the wrong end of binoculars. I began to have dreams of some of the people I had met in the village when we patrolled outside the Ky Ha peninsula, their faces torn apart by my tracers arching down from the sky as I felt torn apart from myself, lines unraveling, drifting form-free, ghost-like. My work seemed absurd. Sometimes I typed reports and requisitions and requests for medals in language that was all hyperbole, that negated by vagueness and exaggeration both the true bravery of the men, and the moral complications of the actions described. Sometimes I stood guard. Occasionally I helped grease the helicopter rotors. I watched and listened to artillery barrages tearing into the invisible countryside around us. A new colonel arrived, trucking in a plane load of appliances for his tent, including a refrigerator. The pilots seemed to look at themselves as figures in a World War Two movie, gave themselves colorful nicknames. Whatever got them through, I thought. Perhaps what I felt was the malaise of occupation troops, though I wouldn't have named it that at the time, and the people we were occupying seemed, for the most part, absent. Vietnamese hootch-maids cleaned the wooden-decked tents and did our laundry, congregating in the early morning in the Quonset hut used for showers and washing the clothing under the showerheads. A lieutenant from my old unit arrived with a small contingent that set up in some tents near the perimeter. He threw a party, had a load of prostitutes trucked in from Hue, took the best-looking two for himself. That was the extent of our connection to the Vietnamese we'd come to save for Democracy: hootch-maids and whores. Some of the men in the unit got in the habit of stripping down and showering while the Vietnamese girls and women were washing clothes, some of the girls no older than twelve. The men wanted to expose themselves. In my kinder moments, I can think of that word, *expose,* as perhaps a need to express their vulnerability. Here I am. Stripped of uniform. A human being. But it wasn't an exposure those girls and women sought; it was an exercise in power over the powerless, an eye-rape. I can do this and there is nothing you can do about it.

Maybe it was both definitions.

Phu Bai was, is, some fifteen miles down Highway One from Hue, the old imperial capital, a place off-limits to American troops, except for a detachment at the American Consular offices there. The highway to the city was The Street Without Joy, a deadly stretch controlled by the Viet Cong. But the idea of Hue, of going to Hue somehow began to obsess me: it was the forbidden country. I felt, though I also wouldn't have expressed it that way at the time, that in being cut off from the Vietnamese, I had been cut off from my own heart. I was in a community outside that heart. I would go to Hue, to Vietnam. I would expose myself. I didn't care if it would kill me. Killing me would save my life.

That was my mood anyway when a friend came to visit the squadron. Tom Campeau was an enlisted Marine combat photographer for the 1st Marine Air Wing information office; he had flown on a mission with me near Khe Sanh. I think I made some excuse to him of needing to go to the consulate in Hue, to get, of all things, a passport—I was not in a logical frame of mind. But Campeau never was either, and we recruited one other boy and with that small fire team we were determined to get to the imperial city.

The three of us put on our full combat gear: helmets, flak jackets, cartridge belts and bandoleers of ammunition, our M-14s, and snuck out of the perimeter, or rather walked out, onto Highway One, as if we knew what we were doing. We were off to see the wizard. We hiked past rice paddies, feeling, not inaccurately, very exposed. A little up the road, we flagged down a small Vietnamese jitney, filled with farmers, their wives and their baskets, and hanging on madly to the back, rode into Hue. The farmers and their wives looked at us in horror: we were making them a target. It was the stupidest thing I had ever done in the war, outside of going to it in the first place.

Finally, the city closed around us, the coolness of the old stone houses pressing in. We were followed everywhere by a wake of astonished looks: three heavily armed Americans suddenly moving along the crowded streets, strolling along the bank of the Perfume River, as if to prefigure the fighting that would take place there a year later. I think that astonishment saved our lives. I think we were seen as a hallucination. I certainly felt that way.

But fate protects the stupid at times, and we survived and returned, but from then on Hue came to represent to me the opposite of the war; my own preserved and complex humanity; a place I could only visit, for now, armed and armored.

\*\*\*

About a year after our visit, Hue was nearly destroyed in the Tet offensive, after regular People's Army and National Liberation Forces at first occupied the city, and then held it for almost a month "until the Marines, bombing and strafing from the air, fighting street by street and house by house, retook the city," writes Marilyn Young in *The Vietnam Wars*. "…Of Hue's 17,134 houses, 9,776 were completely destroyed; 3,169 seriously damaged." The ancient city streets we'd walked were reduced to rubble. My friend Ehrhart was wounded in that battle. My friend Duc's father, a South Vietnamese government official, was taken prisoner, sent North to disappear for years. Thousands died, and after the fighting, many shallow, trenched graves were found, the people in them had had their hands bound, and were either shot in the head of buried alive. Official U.S. reports claimed that between 2,800 to 5,700 Saigon government officials and their supporters were executed. Official Democratic Republic of Vietnam claim there were none. Examining all of the different, contradictory reports and stances, Young concludes that "There is little question that there were executions [by the NLF] in Hue, both in the initial stages of the occupation and in the last days of the battle there," though—while stating that it is "unseemly, even obscene, to argue about the numbers"—she tends to place the figure of those killed in the hundreds rather than the thousands, and claims some of the executions were done by Saigon government squads killing NLF supporters who had revealed themselves during the occupation. Yet "....what the history of Tet in the city of Hue reveals", Young writes, "is the extraordinary harshness and brutality of a struggle that had been going on for over twenty years."

The conflicting histories of Hue, intolerant of each other's existence, contain the conflicting histories of the war itself; the need for new dichotomies.

\*\*\*

That evening, I walked along the Perfume River, along the same way I'd come all those years before. Then I went to the Hue railroad station and met the train from Ho Chi Minh City. My son was on it, stepping down to be in Hue for the second time in his life, as I had done earlier that day, coming to be with me in the city I'd first come to searching for some kind of peace, when I was but a little younger than he was now.

Wayne Karlin

Letter

to a North Vietnamese soldier
whose life crossed paths with mine
in Hue City, February 5th, 1968

Thought you killed me
with that rocket? Well, you nearly did:
splattered walls and splintered air
knocked me cold and full of holes,
and brought the roof down on my head.

But I lived,
long enough to wonder often
how you missed, long enough
to wish too many times
you hadn't.

What's it like back there?
It's all behind us here,
and after all those years of possibility,
things are back to normal.
We just had a special birthday,
and we've found again our inspiration
by recalling where we came from
and forgetting where we've been.

Oh, we're still haggling over pieces
of the lives sticking out
beyond the margins of our latest
history books—but no one haggles
with the authors.

Do better than that
you cock-eyed gunner with the brass
to send me back alive among a people
I can never feel
At ease with anymore:

*remember where you've been, and why,*
*And then build houses; build villages,*
*dikes and schools, songs*
*and children in that green land*
*I blackened with my shadow*
*And the shadow of my flag.*

*Remember Ho Chi Minh*
*was a poet: please*
*do not let it all come down*
*to nothing.*

W.D. Ehrhart

# SCENE FOUR
## Killing Love:
## 2000

# KILLING LOVE

After the shoot, I sit for a time with Michael, still conscious of the picture we must be making: middle-aged man speaking to younger self. I had picked him from among the extras because he was around my height, more slender than I—which of course was right—and had the right color eyes. Jonathan and Binh had hired an actor for the part, but he had never shown up. There had been another possible match also, but that boy didn't speak English. Michael did, though he was from Spain.

It is hot and the humidity is high and as we speak, the crew preparing the site for the next shot, he strips off the helmet and flak jacket. He taps out a cigarette, and lights it, sighs, the smoke trailing from his nostrils. I ask him what he is doing in Vietnam.

"I've been motorcycling through Asia."

"Beautiful bike," I say. I'd seen him drive up on it that morning: a 750cc Moto Guzzi. "A little big for Vietnam."

"It draws crowds," he nods.

"How long have you been in Vietnam."

"About three months now. Longer than I expected to be."

"It happens."

"Yes, it happens," he says, in a way that invites me to ask what. Before I can, Nguyen Ho comes over and sits on a rock next to us, sets down his camera. He is a man of about my age, another NVA veteran: he works for Hanh, and was on set to do a making-of film documentary, as in "The Making of *Song of the Stork*," Hanh's idea. Michael offers him a cigarette.

"What happens?" Ho asks.

"A girl," Michael says.

Ho and I look at each other and smile the patronizing smiles of veterans of a different kind of war.

"No, not like that," Michael says, touching the artificial mole he'd been given to match the real one on my cheek. "Well, something like that. There was love. But not like that."

He had met the girl, he tells us, at Do Son beach.

"Ah," Ho and I say, in unison.

"No, it was not like that," Michael says again.

Do Son is a resort, a beach town on a peninsula that juts into the sea just below Ha Long Bay, north of Haiphong. Formerly a retreat for French colonialist families, it was a vacation destination for many Hanoians in the summer months, a beautiful spot, but its palm-lined beachfront is crusted now with cheap hotels, massage places, and karaoke bars. It contained, also, a thriving prostitution industry. Michael had met his girl, Tuyet, in a brothel. She was young, pretty; he became a repeat customer. He sensed a tragedy that would give him a chance to be a Redemptive Figure. He started by being gentle with her in bed. By trying to meet her needs. He wouldn't be the kind of customer he knew she must be used to. Come in, undress, use her, leave. He would show her what sex could be like. What tenderness could be like. He went down on her: why should he have all the pleasure? He would show her that no matter how many had used it, her body was still precious to him. His eyes filled with tears at his own compassion. Eventually she told him her story. She was a village girl from a remote area; her mother had been in the Youth Volunteer Brigades during the war. Afterwards she and the others in her battalion were sent as a labor team to that part of the country. There had been no men available, except for the male cadre in charge of the battalion: he impregnated her and several of the other women. Her mother had remained in that area, but was desperately poor, and ill now as well, with a dozen maladies from her

82

wartime service, including a lung condition common to Agent Orange victims. When Tuyet was fifteen, a man had come to the village, recruiting girls for Do Son. She found of course that she didn't make the money he had promised. And she hadn't known she would have to sleep with so many men, each day. But she had clothing, and she was able to send money and medicines home to her mother. That was the most important thing.

Michael's heart melted. He felt he had done what few Westerners had ever done: had opened the secret heart of Asia. It wanted his help. It needed him. He would save this girl, this one precious human being, and in turn would save himself. He would love this girl, who so many would scorn or look down upon, and in doing so, would become a better human being. Listen, he told her. I can get you out of this. Come with me. To Hanoi. I'll give you money for your mother, every month—the sum she'd told him in dong would be no more than fifty dollars a month—and you can get your life together.

Tuyet agreed. She seemed suddenly feverish with enthusiasm, caught up in the romance of the idea. But they wouldn't let her leave with him, she said. She was in debt to her pimp; all the girls were. The house was locked; the girls weren't allowed out unescorted; there was a thug who watched the front door. It was even better than Michael thought.

That night he drove his Moto-Guzzi into the alley next to her window. She opened it, dropped a bundle of her clothing to him, and then dropped herself. He put her on the back of the bike, and took off like Young Lochinvar, her arms wrapped around his waist, her face pressing against his back, her hair flying in the wind like the flag of their love.

Ho, listening, shakes his head.

As Michael speaks, I think of my own trip to Do Son, the year before. I'd gone with my co-editors in Vietnam, the writers Ho Anh Thai and Le Minh Khue, and Vien, a friend of Thai's who had just come back from ten years working in Russia. We had gone to visit a writer, Doan Le, who Thai and Khue—given names come last in Vietnamese—had been telling me about for a long time. She was a novelist, short story writer, but also a poet, a film-maker, and a painter. Her divorce, when her husband fell in love with another woman, had been highly public, and her sister had written a ballad about their break up that had become a popular song in Vietnam. She and Doan Le had left Hanoi and built a house on the edge of the town, against the mountains: many Hanoians, tired of the city, had ex-urbanized themselves there.

She also, it turned out, had started and was running a counseling and rehabilitation program for young prostitutes, to help them get out of the life. As we stood in her living room, she had unveiled a life-sized painting she had done of one of the girls: nude, her eyes defiant, her hair fanned around her head in a way that would later put the picture of Tuyet's hair streaming behind her like a flag as she rode on Michael's Moto Guzzi into my mind. But she was surrounded by ripped, broken lilies, so that somehow you sensed the defiance was bravado, a necessity to protect the fragility you suddenly saw in the face. If he'd known of Doan Le's program, I thought, Michael could have brought Tuyet to her.

We had gone to Do Son in December. There were no tourists at that time of year, and the beachfront restaurants and cafes were empty, the wind from the sea blowing through them. The town was empty in only the way places that are at other times filled with people can be empty, inhabited with the ghost-filled silence left in a house when the family that has lived there for years departs. It was beautiful then to walk under the trees along the beach in that echoing wastage. The sea was as gray and cold and heavy as the sea that would lap at some Northern European town, and along the beach there were tree-shaded, pastel-colored villas that had been built during the French occupation. Across the street from them was a large, grotesque, pink-wedding cake of a hotel: a sign in front of it offering "Thai Massage." When we walked by, the girls would be clustered in front of a door, sitting on the steps, combing each others' hair, listening to radios, bored. When they saw me, their eyes would light for a moment, and they'd smile, until I'd walk past and the masks would dissolve into indifference.

We walked all over Do Son, following the serpentine road that went up the spine of the peninsula, into the thickly forested hills called Cuu Long Son, The Nine Dragons, stopping to drink green tea at a thatch-roofed café perched on the edge of a high cliff, swigging from the bottle of vodka Vien carried everywhere. In the town, Bao Dai, the French-appointed emperor of Vietnam had built one of his innumerable palaces. We had bombed it during the war, but it had been restored and one could stay there now. The central building was no more luxurious than a large, upper middle-class American home, but the grounds, overlooking the town and the western bay of the promontory were lovely, and guest rooms and a restaurant with a water-view terrace had been added. The house was full of portraits of the family—Bao Dai and his wife rigid and bejeweled in emperor and empress clothes—and the emperor's toys, including a teak sweat box.

I told Khue, Thai, and Vien a story I'd read about Bao Dai that underscored his awareness that his job as emperor, and the benefits that came with it, depended on being a good puppet for the French. At one point, he had in his entourage a French blonde whose real job everyone knew, but who was officially called an actress, in the "imperial film unit." When Bao Dai heard one of his other friends ridiculing her, he said: "She is only doing her job. I'm the real whore."

"It's only history to us," Thai said, as we looked into the throne room. For the equivalent of about $7.00 in dong, you could have your photo taken on Bao Dai's throne, in his clothing—or in the empress's, if you wished. For about $70, you could sleep in their bed. "For another $70, you can fuck the queen's ghost," Vien said.

At the other end of the peninsula, the Vietnamese, in partnership with a Hong Kong syndicate, had built a large, tacky gambling casino. We walked up the hill to it, though we'd been told Vietnamese weren't allowed inside. The parking lot was filled with buses from China, from where most of the patrons come. Come on, I said, we'll just look inside.

The entrance hall was carpeted. A girl stood behind bars in a ticket booth-type window on the right side. On the other side was an entrance leading, from the noise of bells, levers, shouts, and laughter, to the gambling. I walked up to the girl. "How much is it to get in?"

She looked at me glumly. "Ten percent," she said, in English.

"Ten percent of what?" I asked.

"Ten percent," she said sullenly.

"Yes. I understand. But ten percent of what?"

"Ten percent!" she screamed.

"Let's go," Thai said. He and Khue were laughing.

I retreated and we walked back down the long slope of the road to the town. Two eagles soared overhead. Ten percent of what? I thought. But I knew.

Ten percent would have been a bargain. It was never only ten percent.

I think of Do Son as Michael tells his story. He stops speaking. He lights another cigarette. He puts the helmet back on, and his face is shadowed beneath it, as he sits across from me, a helmeted, flak-jacketed, muddy apparition.

"That was very foolish," Ho says. Jonathan comes over and sits down next to me.

"I suppose," Michael says.

"It turned out badly," Ho says confidently.

Michael nods. He had gotten Tuyet back to Hanoi, installed her in the one-room flat he'd rented. They stayed for a month. He gave her money to send to her mother, as he'd promised. He told her they would work out their relationship—he wasn't her jailer. But she was afraid to leave the house. Afraid that the people to whom she owed money would snatch her.

Ho points at Michael. "You need to be afraid of them also, do you understand?"

He nods. He knows. But then she had seemed to get restless. A little irritable. She complained that he didn't know how to buy the food she needed, but when he suggested she go shopping, or they go together, she accused him of wanting to put her in danger. In bed, she seemed indifferent, or angry. Then, when he came back one day from market, the room was empty, Tuyet and her things gone. He was afraid now; afraid they had found her, afraid what they would do to her. He imagined her locked away, abused, tortured by gangsters. He felt responsible. He had made promises to her, she had believed him, relied on his protection. Now she was paying for it.

"I don't know what to do now," he says. "I can't just leave her. It's...*como matar el amor*. Like killing love. She haunts me."

*Como matar el amor.* It is a phrase only a Southern European or Latin American could get away with. Ho and I look at each other, thinking the same thing: she'd gotten bored and left. But he'd put too much into his belief, his mission of redemption, and we both thought it too cruel to say what is on our minds. A phrase Forrest had said to me on the plane comes back to me now, another essential he'd grasped that I'd thought banal at the time. *It's all sex gone bad.* Killing love.

"There's a movie," I say to Jonathan, later.

"Been done-la," he sighs.

INT/DAY EMPEROR RESTAURANT, HA NOI
Van, middle aged, and Old John at a table. Van opens
the returned diary, runs his finger over the page.

VAN
Thank you, John. You have given me back a missing part
of my life.

JOHN
(Touches book). This was a part of my life for thirty
years. Every time I saw it, I remembered that day. I
wrote my own poetry in it. Now that's yours, just like
your poetry became part of me.

VAN
(Riffling pages, finds one poem. Smiles in recognition.)
When I wrote this poem, I didn't know I would almost
be dead in the next moment. Strangely enough, it was a
poem about coming home. About love.

JOHN
Yes. I know. I think, in a sense, that's what all my war
poems have been about.

VAN
About love?

JOHN
*Como matar el amor.* You bet.

Wayne Karlin

The Last Poem in Van's Captured Diary

*The Mandarin Scholar Returns*

*When he returns to*
*His green city*
*Will it be as the famous*
*Scholar-husband, the mandarin-to-be*
*Who, having passed his exams*
*Rides home like an emperor,*
*His name written on the shining*
*Board lacquered in red and gold*
*His minions calming the excitement*
*Of the crowds?*

*So our songs are sung, my countrymen,*
*So much do we value wisdom and learning*
*So highly will we value the wisdom*
*He will bring back to enrich now*
*His village His green city*
*The knowledge he has found that*
*Men seek with their deepest heart*

*Of how to kill their deepest heart*
*Of how flesh parts easily as water*
*But never flows back to its form*
*Of how to wrap themselves in*
*Trung Quan leaves*
*So they can watch untouched as*
*The earth and its flesh is consumed*
*O what knowledge he will bring back*
*To his green city, to the fragrance of*
*His bridal bed,*
*this scholar, this mandarin-to-be.*

*Quang Tri, 1968*

John's First Poem in Van's Captured Diary

*Back in the World*

*Tell me again about Troy,*
*Penelope says,*
*Still knitting his shroud*
*As Telemachus makes a face*
*And tries on a new robe*
*And the courtiers nudge each other*
*And grin*
*And cover their yawns with soft palms*
*Their manicured fingers*
*Fluttering*
*And he can see in their eyes*
*They don't believe.*

*Men could sit in the dark*
*Waiting to be devoured by*
*A monster who would tear*
*Their limbs and rip their faces*
*With his rotten teeth*
*Splinter their bones into*
*Razoring shards that would*
*Fly through the dark*
*Like beaked fury*
*To slice the light out of others*
*And leave yet others alive*
*Out of no virtue but chance.*

*Or that men yearning for*
*Home and hearth and the*
*Touch of woman and child*
*Could tear down walls*
*And burn homes and*
*Rend the flesh they held*

*Mirrored in their own hearts*
*As if punishing themselves*
*For having hearts.*

*Or would burn a city and its children*
*Out of a dream of freedom and love.*

*Or that a man could come home*
*Naked and dripping out of the sea*
*With a funeral pyre still*
*Burning in his flesh.*

*And Odysseus knew then*
*He had come to the Land*
*Of the Lotus Eaters.*

# LUCK

The two girls rise from the stream, laughing and splashing, their white t-shirts clinging to, revealing, their breasts. Which, I suppose, is the idea. We are upstream from the village, in a small grove of bamboo and linden trees, overlooking the water. The POV is from our bank: two of the actors playing the young North Vietnamese soldiers May and Manh are sitting, relaxing, when they spot the girls—members of the Youth Volunteer Brigades—bathing, and spy on them.

The Vietnamese boom operator is having trouble holding the mike close enough to the actors' mouths without getting it into the shot. His Australian boss is swearing at him steadily. "You set?" Jon calls. "O.K! Quiet!" Binh echoes the call in Vietnamese. As if on cue, the villagers who have crowded into another grove across a small gully, began muttering. "Shut those fooking people up!" The Australian screams. He snatches the mike from his assistant. "Like this, you fooking idjit," he yells. "Hold it up. Keep it out of the camera box. Jon, can we please kill those people now?" He waves at the villagers.

"Only the women and children," Jon said, staring at him. "Especially the children. They make all the noise."

"Waste the bleeding little buggers," the Australian says. "Did anybody bring the M-16s?"

Binh runs over to the bank and screams at the villagers. Hanh comes up next to him, with a megaphone. She speaks sternly, a tiny general addressing her troops, and the crowd subdues. The girls are still splashing each other in the muddy water, oblivious.

Jon grins, shakes his head. "Wet women," he says. "That's what this film needs. Some wet, wet women."

That night I went to my friend Ho Anh Thai's house for dinner. When I opened the door, Thai was standing there, grinning at me and shaking his head. "Mr. American Man," he said, and we embraced. Le Minh Khue was standing next to him. "*Lao Gia,*" she said, tapping my forehead with her finger. Old man. We grinned at each other, as we always did, with a certain triumphant glee, as if our friendship was a joke we'd managed to pull on the deadly capriciousness of the world.

Thai's teenage niece, Huyen My, took my hand and she clung to me as I sat down, telling me about her day as quickly as she could, as if she wanted to get everything out before the adults took me, or before the old man passed away. Her name meant "Homely," following the Vietnamese custom of warding off malevolent and jealous *ma,* spirits, by giving beautiful children uninviting names. "You have an admirer," Khue said, and I put my arm around My's shoulders. "She's my girl." My beamed. She had her mother's smile: a look of permanent amazed delight that things had turned out the way they had. She was a comfortable and secure child, and seemed to lack the sense one sometimes had of American adolescents that they lived in a different country than their parents. Looking around, I felt something relax in me, something I hadn't known I'd been clenching deep inside until I'd come here.

I saw Le Minh Khue looking at My. Khue had been sixteen, a year younger than My, and her own daughter, Phuoc, when she'd gone into the Youth Volunteer Brigades to help maintain the Ho Chi Minh Trails under our bombing, and watching her gaze, I thought I knew what she was feeling. She understood what young flesh and spirit didn't understand about itself: how the world could rend and shred it. Khue had watched girlfriends die next to her, watched a river of young men flow down the Trail, going south to the war, watched the dead and wounded sometimes—when they weren't heaped in nameless graves—flow back in a counter-wash, and at times, also, held the wounded in her arms while they died and then helped to build their coffins and bury them, so that by the time she was seventeen, long before she'd given birth to her own daughter, she had held many other children in her arms as they slipped from the world, calling for their mothers. Khue smiled often and completely and loved to laugh, but her eyes held a depth of sadness that would drown you if you looked into them too long.

When we sat down at the table, I told her about the bathing scene we'd shot, built around the idea that the girls were flirting, knew the soldiers were watching and were trying to entice them.

"Is that how it was?"

She made a face at me. "Eat first," Thai's sister-in-law, Chan Phuong said. "Talk later. My, let go of uncle's arm." Thai's brother, Ho Anh Tai—a name which followed the Vietnamese custom of warding off baffled foreigners with impossibly close tonal differences—opened a bottle of snake wine. "You remember this?" Tai said. He poured; only he and I were drinking it. The tabletop was covered with a platoon in formation of Heineken and Tiger beer cans: inevitable with any Vietnamese meal to which guests were invited.

"You'll never let me forget," I said. Khue poured a beer, and then poured for Thai, My, and Thang Long, the ten-year-old. His name was the ancient name for Hanoi. Khue raised her glass. "To the movie star."

"*Cam on,*" I said. Thank you.

"'*The Song of the Stork,*'" Thai pronounced. "Why that title?"

"It's from one of your old fables. A female stork finds

herself in a trap. When the peasant comes along, she tells him: 'when you cook me, be sure to use clean water.' I'm not quite sure of the meaning," I admitted.

"Then you're perhaps not quite so Vietnamese. Who are the actors?"

"Quang Hai is in it." Thai had introduced me to the young actor the year before.

"Ah, yes? Good."

"And his wife, Hai Yen."

"Beautiful, yes? The Exquisite Hai Yen."

"Yes. The Exquisite Hai Yen. And Pham Ba, Nguyen Ngoc Hiep, Ta Ngoc Bao, and Tran Mai Nugyen."

"Well, it's a good group."

Chan Phuong began bringing dishes to the table: a shrimp soup, tofu, a water cress salad, spring rolls, rice and fish sauce, beef strips, fried chicken, cut into small cubes. The last dish was a chicken in chili sauce. "What's the name of this?" I asked Khue, and she said something I didn't understand. Everyone else at the table laughed. I looked at Thai.

"She said for Americans it's called 'eat and immediately shit'."

"Lovely. I thought that's what you gave me last time."

Chan Phuong poked her chopsticks at me threateningly.

"What I like about Khue," Tai said, grinning, "is the element of surprise. She looks very sweet and speaks softly, with femininity. But then she can swear and laugh like a man."

"I agree," I said, my mouth full. It was what I liked also. The complications of someone I'd have once seen as a target.

Khue had just turned fifty that year, but I'd seen photos of her in her floppy jungle hat when she'd been a Youth Brigade volunteer, a sixteen-year-old trudging down the Ho Chi Minh Trail with a rucksack bulging with books by the American authors she loved: Hemingway, Steinbeck, London. I would always try, and fail, to imagine what lessons in grace under pressure she could draw from those authors who shared the nationality of the men dropping bombs around her, though I suppose there's a kind of romanticized, transcendent hope in that idea. Her face across the table from me was the same now as it had been in that photo, except for the smile lines around her mouth and a crinkling web around her eyes, a slight broadening of her cheeks. It was the kind of face that got more interesting as it got older, the way women's faces weren't supposed to. She was beautiful with her history. If you knew that history and looked into her eyes, they broke your heart, and if you didn't know it, they broke your heart anyway, and you didn't know why, only that they were stained with an indelible sadness that made her smile and laughter seem deeply earned. Early in the war, the village where she was staying had been bombed, wiped out, and at times I would wonder how she could look at me without seeing that fire, though a few months later, after I'd gone home and our own buildings and sense of invulnerability suddenly disappeared in flame and dust, she wrote to me with words of commiseration and advice about how to bear it, and I was not surprised that she had left out what she might have said.

"That's not true!" she said to Tai. She punched me in the arm. "I'm very nice. What you said about the girls isn't true either. We would never bathe like that, if we knew the men were around. We didn't entice."

"I don't know. Your stories about the war, about life on the Ho Chi Minh Trail are realistic—I mean, for when they were written, there's no propaganda, and the characters you draw seem real, three-dimensional. But it always seems to me you leave out two things: sex and death. I know there had to have been death. And with all those young people, boys and girls together, around so much death, I'd hope there was also some love-making."

"Writers couldn't write then about sex or death—at least not the dead from our side," Thai said.

"I know, I know. But I can't extract one from the other,

not when I write about the war." Forrest's words came back to me again. "It always seems tied to bad sex, love turned inside out."

Khue snorted, raised her eyebrow mockingly, as if to ask: what's your agenda? I was used to that also. She regarded everything I said with complete skepticism. She was the same way with everyone, though she'd only show it openly to her friends. It was the way she looked at the world: as if any seemingly innocent meter of it could contain unexploded bombs.

"We were all beautiful," she said. She reached over, ran her fingers through My's back-length hair. "And all innocent. Like ice cream cones. There was no sex. None at all. Yes, that's right. We were all innocent as ice-cream cones."

"Ice-cream cones?"

"*Lau gia*," she said, "you're the type who, when you see the naked statues in museums, only sees sex."

"Sure, that's me, why not? That's what uncovered bodies suggest. The problem isn't seeing sex instead of beauty. It's seeing sex as unbeautiful," I said earnestly.

She looked disgusted. "*Chieu oi*," she said, shaking her head. "My God, listen to that, would you!" She was grinning.

Then she wasn't. Her eyes had suddenly depthed with sorrow, and she shook her head, looking at me, as if to say: is that all you really see when you see the shapes flesh can take? Ah, *lau gia*, how lucky you are.

*Out-take: The American Reader*

The first time Mai sees Americans they are bathing in a stream about a thousand meters from where she and two of her girl friends lay watching through the foliage. The soldiers' voices don't carry that far, though she can see they are splashing, probably laughing, their skin occasionally flashing like daylight through the leaves. She wishes she could get closer, but if Ninh, the male section leader, knows they have even gotten this close, they will all be in trouble.

She wants to see them in their flesh: the enemy—still held tightly shut against the very shattering they would bring her in the tattered books she carries in her rucksack. Her aunt's treasures, given to Mai when she had joined the Volunteers, gone South to keep open the Trail that knit the Nation. Her aunt a teacher and a good revolutionary and the authors approved for good revolutionaries, but sometimes after a bombing or strafing, the other girls would look at Mai with bitter astonishment. The American reader. The adjective edging resentfully into a noun. Yet there is always a wistfulness in their teasing as well. As if what Mai is holding onto is something they can't name but feel sliding out of themselves as well, day by day.

She strains to see the Americans through the screen of leaves. They are still Tom Joad, moving towards a vision of a perfected, kind world, as she, when she remembers, imagines herself doing, moving through the dust of a space she finds unimaginable in the closeness of the jungle—even though they seem now to be trying to turn that jungle, those trees, into that same bowl of dust and emptiness Joad had fled to a greener land. They are Robert Jordan, laying on his stomach, watching the bridge, as she lays on her stomach, watching Jordan's compatriots now, and she is Marie, waiting in the encompassing warmth of his sleeping bag, for the warmth of flesh and connection against the coldness of death. They are a man trying with his hands to build a fire as the circle of howling wolves closed in on him, as her own hands, her fingers, worked frantically to prevent the fire blossoming from the guts of the bomb that moments before had howled down from them to her; they are the machines that come to kill her and hers; they are the red flashing of tracers through the jungle canopy, the masked, mirroring face hovering above, the sudden light shivering like panic through the branches. They are torn apart in her mind and she needs to knit them together if she is going to knit herself together. They are a weight in her rucksack, the books that anchor her; they give her paths she can follow along the paths she must follow; they give her the courage to face themselves. They are these naked boys in a jungle pond, though they are too far away to really see anything, her friend complains in a whisper, and the other two girls giggle. They are too far away to see anything, she thinks, because they are ghosts, they are lines in a book, they are too many contradictions to be real, to be flesh, to be naked.

They are flying over Helicopter Valley, with its cupped wreckage, when the pilot, DeLeon's, scream pierces John's ears, a sound so filled with terror and despair that, filtered through earphone static, he hears it as a wail spiraling up from the broken aircraft below them. The helicopter jerks, up and then down. He traverses the ground with the barrel of the machine gun. He sees no tracers, has heard nothing hit the plane. He risks a glance over at the two prisoners they'd picked up at LZ Crow, drags the flashed afterimage of them quickly back to his stare out of the port. The recon Marine sitting across from them hadn't moved. His M-14 on his lap, his finger on the trigger. The two in olive-green North Vietnamese Army uniforms tattered, muddy and bloody, but not faded. New guys. Sitting motionless also, the base of a triangle, the recon Marine the apex, their eyes dulled, heads leaning towards each other, side by side, as if still fastened together by the wire the Nungs who had captured them had punctured through their cheeks. The Marine—he was a staff sergeant—had cursed and pulled it out when they'd been handed over, the two North Vietnamese jerking like fish as he did it. The holes in their cheeks scabbed over now, but still bleeding red slick snail trails down their swollen cheeks. Tears from strange eyes. The staff sergeant's eyes dulled also, head tilted.

The noise from the cockpit—curses, scuffles—hasn't abated. Sam keys his mike: "Sir, what's happening?"

"A fucking snake," the co-pilot, Anderson says, his voice more exasperated than fearful.

A *snake*, he says again, indignantly, and the word, the hot, poisonous *sibilance* of it, opens into Everything. Into the jagged carpet of smashed helicopters below them. Into the impossible, malevolent, steambath of tangled, vine-strangled, insect-crawling, breezeless, lightless at midday, hundred-foot tall triple-canopy jungle they were over again now. Into the men they'd set down in it and taken out, sucked dry like insects caught in a web. Into clouds of hot, red laterite dust sucked into engines at take-off, the nerve-racking dance of hands and feet on collective and cyclic and pedals, a manic weave on the loom of the very centrifugal force that wants to tear the thousands of pieces of machinery to pieces; into landing too hot and too heavy and downwind on slopes picketed with trees, the heavy wet air pushing down the helicopter loaded with its weight of flesh and equipment, all the deadly specific numbers: thirteen grunts times eighty pounds each of steel helmets, M-14s, web belts hung with grenades and loaded magazines and full canteens and entrenching tools and machetes and flak jackets and field packs, not to mention the M-60 machine guns or mortars the weapons platoons carried, not to mention the 150 to 200 pound eighteen to twenty year old bodies carrying all of it, not to mention the helicopter's own machine guns and ammunition and flak-jacketed crew and 2200-pounds-of-fuel, all optimal conditions needed to suck the lift right from under blades, to wind down, as if it were the clock of your life, the RPM that kept you in the air; to stop rotor blades like a hand stuck into a fan, to feel yourself a gracefully floating dandelion suddenly puffed on from above by a malevolent hot-breathed giant, to be slammed into the terrain below, into other helicopters, into screaming men and suddenly liberated fifty foot-long blades slicing through air foliage torsos necks heads arms and later you come down and see someone still sitting behind a log as if taking a break and you pick up what turns out to be only the top half of a sergeant, lighter that way, and yes, a clean-cut boy, you think. It's all there, in those words, in the utterly appropriate hissed curse of them: The12.7mm North Vietnamese anti-aircraft guns and B-40 rockets and quad-fifty machine guns that send orange and green fireballs streaking past the ports, and the ship you'd watched go down yesterday, thick black smoke streaming from the fuel line the incendiary round had hit, smashing into the ridge, rolling on its back, bursting into flames, a random pyre auto-rotating frantically as if to blow out its own flames before twisting over, breaking its rotored back on the ground, the sheet of flame moving through the compartment, the two men jumping out of the back, one too high, to his death; the other too low, the flaming mass falling on top of him, and the rest all gone by then, burning bright in that forest of eternal night. And, if that wasn't enough, there were the prisoners dragged to the rear ramp like fish flopping on a wire, and the grenade your allies from the Army of the Republic of Vietnam Itself had left wedged under a red-webbed seat, and the wounded and dead you'd scooped out of the black meat-grinding, fire-seared night. And if, just in case, by any chance, as Vietnam would have it, to top it all, if that wasn't enough, then you could still have a fucking snake in your cockpit.

She looks at her friends, Suong and Thu Ha, their faces shaded under the floppy green jungle hats, but scratched, smudged, hollow-cheeked with hunger, gums bleeding, teeth loose. If she could see their bodies under the clothes that hung like rags on them, she would see ribs pushing against paper-thin flesh over stomachs bloated with hunger, nets of scars and scratches, insect bites and scabies. They are all like that. She understands what bodies are. She understands the hungers, shares them; they are all young, girls and boys, and they breath and sleep with death as if they are old, and they want their lives, and they all understand a life can be folded like an endless cloth into ten minutes that you can slowly draw back out and touch and savor all the rest of your life, however long it goes on from that moment. When bodies are laid out on the broken earth they look like part of it. People go South dressed and they come back dead, and that direction itself has come to mean death, and she helps bury them, the dead, though sometimes they are wounded and sometimes she holds them, the way the woman in Steinbeck held the starving man against her breast and gave him suck, and they call her mother, though she's younger than them, and she remembers how, in her village, before she'd gone South, the bombs had struck before the time people knew they needed to build shelters and she'd come back from the school outing to see the bodies huddled under the trees, mothers and fathers with children clutched and melted to their chests. And sometimes they are the other girls or boys from her unit, and often the bombs blast the clothing from their bodies so they go into their deaths as they had come into their births and she had at first, more than death itself, feared that exposure. But she is seventeen now and she knows that death makes everyone sexless. In a line of bodies, what caught your eye was how little difference there was, how easily it could be erased. Her thoughts are scrambled, confused, and mixed now with the dim white figures seen through the screen of leaves, the ghosts that would kill her.

"Where, sir?" John says nervously, keying his mike. He is hearing curses, scrambling noises through the earphones. "Shit," DeLeon says, his voice high-pitched.

"No joy, no joy," Anderson says. No visual contact.

"It went behind the instrument panel!"

"Are you sure?" Anderson's voice. "I think it's a fucking viper."

*I'm de vindow viper.* Punch line of an old joke. John looks down nervously at his feet. Sweat rolls down his neck, under the collar of his flight suit, crawls down his back; he wants to turn, search, raise his legs, dance like a mad bagpiper. He feels his skin contracting under the leg of his flightsuit, his muscles spasming up to his thighs. Snake crawl. *I'm de bamboo viper.* He thinks of it sliding behind the HAC and co-pilot, through the hatch, under the web seats, or along the wiring over his head. Hears, suddenly, the voice of the flight commander, Colonel Watson in his ICS, asking them what the problem is.

The helicopter had reared out of formation—they are flying in a division, four helicopters—when DeLeon let go of the collective. The pilot had pulled out his survival knife and hacked at the snake, which had dropped heavily to the deck, shot like an arrow between Anderson's rubber foot pedals into the tangle of wires behind the instrument panel. Straightened up and slithered off, John hears DeLeon say, with the near-hysterical hilarity which means, John knows, that the incident has already become a war story, will be told everywhere, was humming through the ether even now.

But the snake is still in the aircraft, had not yet crawled into the safety of story. For all he knows it is still coiled around wires behind the panels, cunning, camouflaging itself as part of the technology, using the machinery of the enemy against the enemy. Low crawling, naked and slick, a sapper coming through the wire. Touched my elbow like a kiss, slid along the aluminum ledge under the window, he hears DeLeon say to Anderson. *I'm the vindow viper.* Green brown in complexion, maybe three foot tall, skinny as a pencil, DeLeon says. He talking to them now. Fanged and dangerous. Find the fucker. Take no prisoners.

"A fucking snake," Anderson says, and John can feel it, sense the snake, moving under the deck plates, sneaking through the avionics. Staying just ahead of or just behind them. He glances down, involuntarily. Something to the left of his left foot. Green and brown. He looks at the staff sergeant. He still hasn't moved, and neither have the prisoners. They're each others' stories too, but they don't know the end yet. John slowly picks up the M-1 carbine he'd bought for ten dollars from an ARVN as a backup weapon. What the hell is he going to do, shoot it through the deck? He slowly leans the carbine against the ammo catcher, slides out his K-bar knife. It seems motionless. Playing dead, he thinks. *I'm the vindow viper and I've come to vipe your vindow.* He stares. He should be looking out of his port. It is getting rapidly dark. But the enemy is here. It's too still. Too…dull. Inanimate. It can't be a snake. He slowly advances the point of the knife, pushes down swiftly. Like a snake striking. The object is solid. Un-snake-like. He slowly squats, thinking *grenade*. No. A small book. He picks it up, impaled, pulls it off the blade, realizing, too late, it may be a booby-trap anyway. No. It doesn't explode. There's a black and white picture of a girl inside, a young couple in front of an iron gate fashioned into a circle of Chinese ideograms. But the writing on the stained pages, cribbed and lined through and smudged and blurring in the waning light, is Vietnamese writing, regular letters tortured top and bottom with little barbed wire spikes. The written lines broken, as if poetry. Probably belonged to one of the prisoners. He should give it to the sergeant. Snake's diary, he thinks. Viper story. The two prisoners and the sergeant are still staring at each other, motionless as a diorama, as if all three have been wired together. The small book burns his hand, through his flight glove, as if it has dripped venom on him. He straightens up, quickly tosses it out of his port. Follows it with his machine gun barrel, twisting and fluttering in the air, white pages winging against dark sky, the photos flying out like released spirits.

It is growing dark, and is darker yet under the thick-knit branches canopied over the creek where she bathes. It is the same pool, a widening of the creek really, where the Americans had bathed. Mai can't see. Knows she can't be seen. Suddenly the noise of rotors beats down on top of the leaves like fists beating on a door, and she freezes until it fades off, leaving only its echoes and then the memory of its echoes. She thinks, taking herself away from it, how she will make all this into story, mix has-been with could-be; fold the story over herself like a camouflage shelter as the bombs fall closer. This urgency to immerse herself in the same water, she thinks, to take the mystery of them into her skin, she thinks, and her mind tries to flee the thought, but she has trained herself to clutch at those fugitives of her being; they were in the end the whispers that named her. She has a broken sliver of soap from a bar that Thu Ha had brought back from Hanoi, a luxury, and she soaps herself, and now she hums the tune to an Italian song all of the girls from Hanoi remember and sing. She has dirt under her nails from the Trail, from the dirt they shoveled back into the craters, smoothing them for the trucks going South, and her fingers stink from the gelignite they'd packed around the bomb she had embraced earlier in the day, helped lower into a hole, blown up. She scrubs her hands and her body, unable to even see her flesh now, feeling herself seeping away, borders dissolving into the water, the darkness, the insect hum. Something heavy and cold and reptilian bumps into her lower belly. She stifles a scream. Reaches out tentatively. Her fingers find hair, a head, a nose, a mouth, and the fear suddenly leaves her, bursting like a bubble opening in water; she knows what this is; it isn't the first time a corpse has come floating down this stream to her. She lets her fingers move along the cold skin, feeling the man's flesh, naked to her own nakedness, feeling his wounds open under her fingertips like kisses, this one lover, from all that had gone South, come back to her now in the dark. She knows what this is, but the Americans she has seen that day come to her mind, and the words she feels written on her back, blurred through her rucksack and into her skin by her sweat, and she lets that thought, lets them, float next to her for a moment, and then lets it go; yes, it could be one of them as easily, and perhaps it is, but it doesn't matter, death doesn't only erase sex, and yes, isn't it pretty to think so.

As the book falls, the helicopter formation wheels west, over the mountainous jungle of the cordillera. A place filled with snakes. The darkness is not so much beginning to cover it as it is entering it, like an injected liquid, the top of the jungle canopy configuring into ominous, fluid shapes. Leaf people. Anderson's voice is in his ear again, his words repeated by DeLeon: they want him and Sam to fire into the fleshy mass below. Into the trees. They think Something is down there. No shit. It's the snake's home. The place of snakes. The home of the snake and the land of the viper. He fires down into it. As he does, he sees an artillery barrage begin, over to the west of their flight path, aircraft diving down, as if called by his fire. A hot shell casing falls on his neck, stings like a snake bite. He fires more, his shoulders shaking, hands vibrating, fires at the ghosts moving under the trees, fires at a girl who bathes with the dead to dream the resurrection of love, who tries to find and frame the face behind the wind and the fire and the noise and the fragmented light. His rounds curve and streak down and the darkling green absorbs them so quickly it is as if they never existed at all.

EXT: DAY, UNDER BANYAN TREE, CAN LO
Old Van and Old John sit and stare at the country.

                    VAN
I always used to dream during the war that some day
we'd build a memorial to the volunteer girls here.

                    JOHN
(Smiles) You wrote a great deal about that dream in your
diary. Sometimes it seemed those girls were the only
thing on your mind.

                    VAN
They were very beautiful. (Both men laugh lightly). We
were all beautiful. Beautiful with death. (He gestures at
the canopy of leaves). As leaves in autumn.

                    JOHN
(Laughs) Poet!

                    VAN
(Echoes John's laugh) And you also, Mr. Famous
American Poet.

                    JOHN
I'm afraid that's your fault. When I opened the diary...I
couldn't read Vietnamese then. But I could see what
you'd written was poetry. It led me both to Vietnamese,
and to poetry.

                    VAN
And to here.

                    JOHN
Yes. The strangeness of that still haunts me. To be
standing on a hill with someone who once would have
killed me; who I would have killed...

VAN

Someone you could have killed. (Looks away. A long pause). Why, John? (they watch the stork flying.) Why didn't you kill me?

JOHN

I wondered when you would ask. If you would ask. It seemed to me you've been afraid to.

VAN

I didn't allow myself to think about it. Not for years.

JOHN

The truth is, I don't know why, Van. You know how crazy a person can get, during combat. It wasn't an act of mercy. My mercy had died long before that. Maybe I was tired of the killing. Maybe I thought you would die anyway. But to be truthful, part of me felt I was killing you anyway. That I was reaching down into you and pulling out your soul. That it was the only way I could continue to live.

VAN

(Shudders. He takes out the diary, thumbs though it, runs his finger over a page) When did you start writing in it?

JOHN

Oh, when I got home. It was as if I had to...continue you. I had never thought of myself as a poet. But it seemed the only way. It was as if your poems bled into mine. Into me.

VAN

(Puts his hand on the tree trunk) Once I was writing a poem. This one (he opens to a page, points) and your planes started bombing us. Some of my friends laid their bodies over mine, so I could finish writing it. (He closes the book, looks at John).

JOHN

I often feel closer to you, to the Vietnamese veterans I've met, then to people in my own country who were not in the war. As if the war is the country we both came from.

VAN

How is it for you? Coming back?

JOHN

Every sight I see, every second is charged, full of weight. I can't see anything for just itself. As it is.

VAN

Standing here in Quang Tri, I feel the same.

JOHN

But yesterday, Van, when we were driving through that pass between the two bamboo covered slopes? All that tangled jungle? I looked up and I thought: a beautiful mountain. And then I realized that during the war I would have hated, feared that place—it was perfect for an ambush. But yesterday, it suddenly just became a beautiful mountain. The war was gone.

VAN

Do you think that's true?

JOHN

Not at all.

# SCENE FIVE
## Fast Forward:
## 2004

# HANDS

Miss Xao seemed very glad to see me. She greeted me as if I were an old friend, or a brother she hadn't seen in years: an effusiveness which left me somewhat puzzled, both because it was the first time I'd ever met her—her real old friend Tran Van Thuy had introduced us—and because I knew that during the war she would have been equally glad to put a bullet in my chest and must have known as well that I would have gladly returned the favor.

After Quang Tri and Hue, Thuy and I had traveled south with the NYU students, over the hump of the Hy Van pass. Before we arrived in Danang though, we detoured out to Xao's village. She had been sitting under the awning of her small, roadside kiosk when we arrived, a large bus suddenly lumbering into view, stopping here in the middle of this nowhere town in Quang Nam, the doors opening, a group of young Americans hung with equipment pouring out onto the dust. There would be no resonance in that image for the kids who immediately surrounded us, but I wondered how Xao and some of the older villagers, watching us now, would take it. A huge smile broke out on her face, awakening the echo of the beauty I'd seen in Thuy's war footage, and when she turned her face and rested it against Thuy's chest as they hugged each other, I half-hoped the side exposed to us would be smoothed again. The wound was not fresh, as it had been in the film we'd seen; the left side of her face was reamed and caved but the wound, over the years, no longer seemed imposed or intruded: it had become part of her.

When Thuy introduced me, she smiled in delight and

embraced me, and then got us sodas. We sat under the thatched awning of the kiosk, and Thuy got her to tell her story, filling in those parts Xao was too modest to talk about. He had first filmed her because she was a legendary National Liberation fighter: a girl known for her beauty and her fierceness and for her deadly accuracy with a rifle. Her father and mother had both been revolutionaries, she said, both killed. When she had seen the Americans coming into her village, she had felt as if her own flesh was being violated. As she said this, she lifted her free hand and caressed her scars, at peace with her wound. The Miss Xao who sat with us seemed completely disconnected from the killer she was describing, not because she felt any regret or lack of pride about her actions—the Americans had come to her country— but because of her soft speech and her gentle smile; because of the way she had taken my hand and we sat with our fingers tightly entwined, as the children of the village and the children we had brought with us, pressed in and heard, for the first time, her story.

After she had been wounded—Thuy told us—she had insisted on being sent back to lead her unit. Her male comrades had wanted her to stay out of the combat then, recover, take a safer job. But she refused, kept fighting, and was finally transferred to a unit that worked undercover in Danang.

Once, when I was at Marble Mountain, some Vietnamese nuns had led us to a cache of mortar rounds hidden in a building not far from the perimeter of the helicopter base. I thought of that now, thought of the times we had been mortared, and I asked her if she had anything to do with that.

You were at that camp? She asked me, and then laughed. Then I would have killed you too.

I looked down at her fingers. They might have pulled the trigger that released the bullet that killed Jim Childers, on his way out of her country. I stared at them, laced with mine now, trigger-finger hooked around trigger-finger.

\*\*\*

In Danang, we stopped at Marble Mountain, and we climbed it, as I'd never been able to do in the war, and from the height the helicopters would sometimes fly, I looked across at the hill where Childers had been killed, and what we did there is a story I'll tell elsewhere in this book. Afterwards we drove south, past Ky Ha and Chu Lai, the road running past my window as the students dozed; the places of my past now pulled reluctantly out of memory and myth and into the present. And then to Son My, the site of the My Lai massacre, a place I had been only in nightmarish contemplation.

Thuy had previously made a documentary film called *The Sound of the Violin at My Lai.* The film does not concentrate solely on that massacre of 500 old men, women and children by American troops. It may have started that way, but Thuy, who always seems to center on the human capacity for grace and redemption in his films, had become fascinated with an American veteran, Mike Boehm, who—although he had nothing to do with the killings in Son My—had formed deep friendships with the Vietnamese and had worked to create a "peace park," and a fund for women in the area who wanted to start businesses. Thuy was impressed that the first time he had seen Mike, the large American had wept when speaking of My Lai, as if by the simple accident of sharing the uniform and the nationality of the men who had done the killing he had taken a very personal responsibility for it; he was touched as well that when he visited Mike's home in the United States he found the American living in a very small, modest, monkish cell of an apartment, with few possessions, his life given over to the redemptive work he was doing. Thuy had always understood—he was too empathetic not to—that the Americans were as human as himself, but he had not expected anyone like Boehm.

When he set out to do the documentary on the occasion of the thirtieth anniversary of the massacre, he found that other Americans had been invited to attend the ceremonies. Hugh Thompson had been the helicopter pilot who, witnessing what was happening on the ground, had landed his helicopter between some American troops and a group of villagers they were about to gun down; his crew chief Glenn Andreotta and his gunner, Larry Colburn, had trained their machine guns that day on their fellow soldiers; they had evacuated people from the area to save them, and later Andreotta had waded into the killing ditch to pull out and save a child. Thirty years later all three crewman—though Andreotta was dead, killed a few weeks later in another battle—were awarded the Soldier's Medal for their actions that day, but only after a campaign initiated by certain officers within the army, who knew that Thompson had turned down a Distinguished Flying Cross offered to him at the time because its citation made no reference to the massacre. The campaign for the award was reinforced by a segment on *Sixty Minutes;* Mike Wallace had plans to bring Thompson and Colburn to My Lai for the thirtieth anniversary: wouldn't it be fitting, the newsman said, if their actions were commemorated before that trip? I was glad they got the medals, but the fact that they were helicopter crew had made them personal heroes to me long before, and in some ways I envied the opportunity they had been given to be tested, to have made the right choices, to have been redeemed.

There were ceremonies that day, and speeches made and incense lit. But Thuy had not been able to find a single connective image that would thread everything together until, talking to Mike Boehm, he found out that the big American played the violin. Thuy's face lit up: if he could get Mike a violin, would he play it here, at My Lai? No need to get one, Mike said. He always carried it with him when he came to Vietnam. He always went places where there had been much killing, where the wandering spirits hung, and played to them.

The final segment of Thuy's film shows him doing just that at My Lai, the violin tucked under his fleshy chin, his large, blunt fingers delicately moving bow across strings, playing taps to soothe the uneasy dead.

When we had filmed *Stork,* the area north of Hanoi had stood in for the battlegrounds in Central Vietnam where Thuy and I had been, but driving through Quang Nam now, I realized again how different the countryside was, the terrain of memory emerging like a suddenly revealed pentimento. On the way to My Lai, we passed by a kind of tori gate for the old base at Chu Lai; there was nothing behind it now but sand flats, an erasure of history I didn't mind at all. I had told our local guide that I'd been at Ky Ha, and he'd also pointed out where a dirt road led into that area, but I had no desire to detour, to drag these sleepy kids with me further into my past. But I was already there. The road to My Lai went past paddies and the mounds of dikes and then into a town. What place is this? I asked the guide. An Tan, he said.

It had been a point with a name on a highway going nowhere, a place we would convoy into, patrol, from Ky Ha, though at the time most of the houses strung along Highway One were fashioned of thatch, corrugated tin sheets discarded by the Americans, and flattened beer cans, and what was now a decent paved road going through it had been rutted dirt, a cloud of yellow dust hanging perpetually over it. A place where I'd received cut number who-knew-what in those thousand cuts Michael Herr mentioned. I'd been standing with some other Marines, armed and wary, in a little shade before a gate made of thorns, buying dusty bottles of soda from the girls who sold them from huge baskets. I joked with one girl who had a dirty face and a beautiful smile; she wanted to try out her American swear words with me, and I was winning hearts and minds, correcting her English: No, say moth-er-fuck-er, not motha fucka. An amtrack—what the Marines called amphibious tractors, and the army called Armored Personnel Carriers, Tracks—clanked to a halt nearby, and the girl ran over and lifted up her basket like an offering to the gods of war. A Marine, deeply sunburned, his utilities and helmet and skin covered with a fine red powder that was reamed on his face with rivulets of sweat, snatched a bottle from the girl, knocked its cap off on the edge of the vehicle, drained the foaming coke. 100 p's, the girl yelled up at him shrilly—the 100 piastres he owed for the drink. He stared at her. 100 p's, she screamed. He threw the bottle at her, hard and fast; she stepped to the side as it whizzed past her head, planted her legs apart, and stared up at him. Her shirt was ragged, held by one button. Her chest was heaving. 100 p's, she insisted. Leave, I thought. Get out of there, kid. The amtrack was scored with bullet rakings, battered, its tracks caked with mud; the men on it staring out with flat indifference or with that crazy grunt-light in their eyes. Leave, I thought. The Marine took out his .45, leaned over the side, and pointed it at the girl's forehead. Di-di, you little gook bitch, he said. Moth-er fuck-er, she said clearly. 100 p's. He cocked the pistol. She didn't move. 100 p's, she said. I understood that she would die before she moved, and I understood that he would blow her away. I didn't move. My M-14 was slung in the reverse way we did so its barrel pointed straight ahead, instead of up over the shoulder, and I remember moving my finger to the trigger. I didn't think of saying anything. Words were meaningless. I remember the wet slick feel of the trigger under my skin; I remember it in my skin. I understood that she would die if I didn't move. We were all frozen in a tableau. His finger was tightening on the trigger, my finger lay on the trigger, the girl's hands gripped the basket. "For shit sake," a voice with a thick, weary Southern accent said from the amtrack, and a skinny Marine leaned over the side and dropped a hundred piaster note to the ground. It fluttered near the girl's feet. She didn't look at it. The other Marine shook his head in disgust, snorted, pulled up the pistol. The girl remained where she was. After a while, she bent down and took the money.

I turned away and went back to my friends. It had been a day when nothing happened. This was not My Lai. This took place at a point called An Tan, on the road to My Lai, where I had never been.

We passed into Quang Ngai province and then stopped in Quang Ngai city, at the crossroads about twelve kilometers before Son My—My Lai was not the real name of the village where the massacre had taken place, but then all Vietnamese names tended to sound alike to us. I sat the students down near a very large, very ancient banyan tree that reminded me of the tree we had filmed under when we did *Song of the Stork*. In the entwined tentacle nests of its roots local people had left clusters of incense sticks, and what seemed to be a small Buddha, though I wasn't sure: it could have been a god or a demon to be placated. It was very hot.

"It's this hot," I said to them. "Maybe hotter. The soldiers who did the killing at My Lai have been called a typical cross-section of American youth. Their average age, I think, was 21. In other words, they're you. They're all male, of course, but we can see from what's happened in Iraq recently, gender may not be a factor." Just before we'd left on the trip, the accounts and photos of the abuses at Abu Ghraib prison had been all over the news; the photo of Lynndie England's face grinning over naked, heaped Iraqi prisoners like a malevolent pixie. "You didn't have a shower last night in a hotel. You've been living in tents, or in holes, and you're sleepless, and you've been walking for days in this heat with seventy pounds of weapons and armor and helmets and packs. The people around you," I waved at a curious cloud of villagers who had come to watch, "sometimes smile, and sometimes you play with their kids, and sometimes they kill you. At least you think it's them. Who else? They speak gibberish, they live in huts. But you never see them. Judd has been killed yesterday when he stepped on a mine. Mark had his balls blown off the day before. Elan lost a leg. Brian was killed by a sniper. Now

119

you've been told you're going into a village where the people who have done this live. You understand you've been told to kill all of them. This is not something of the moment, in other words, some incident or culmination of incidents that sets you off in a murderous rage. You understand you have been told to do this. You go there; you see there is no enemy fire, that there are only old men, women and children in the village. But you've been told to do this. You will do it. Over the next four hours you will kill over 500 people. Some of you will do it reluctantly. Some of you will herd the people systematically into a ditch and do it conscientiously, methodically, just carrying out your orders. Some of you will feel that you have been given the freedom of a god or a devil. You will kill with rage, laughing; you will rape young girls in front of their families, slit open their vaginas, kill their families. You will scalp, cut out tongues. Some of you will not participate. Some will refuse. One will shoot himself in the foot rather than participate.

"So my question to you here, now, is what would you do?"

Silence.

I have given this little speech before to students, and silence is usually the response, as it should be. Is this a fair question? I'll ask them next, and the response is always a somewhat relieved, No, of course not; how could we know what we would do?

"O.K, then what should you do?"

Silence.

"That's the point," I said. "Most of the men who participated didn't know what they should do. There were people there—and afterwards—who resisted. They resisted the power of authority; they resisted peer pressure, they resisted the pressure to be loyal, and to fit in; they resisted the fear that they might be killed themselves; they resisted a cynical acceptance of the evil nature of things. They knew it was wrong and they resisted; they didn't take the choice that would have ruined them. They brought something, no, two things, with them to My Lai that the others didn't have."

"What was that?" Brian asked. He was a blond, handsome boy; a Rockwell picture, and it was easy to imagine a face like his in Charley Company that day—not because it was a killer's face, but just the opposite.

"They knew what they would do because they knew what they should do. And had the strength to do it. Or in this case, to not do it."

"But none of them tried to stop it," Jonathan, one of the Viet Kieu kids said.

"That's true. It took the helicopter crew, people outside their unit, to actively try to stop it. But think if all of them, or even more of them, had just refused to shoot. Harry Stanley, one of the guys who did refuse said, 'Ordering me to shoot down innocent people, that's not an order—that's craziness to me, you know. And so I don't feel like I have to obey that.' What if more people had said that?"

"It wouldn't have happened," Vanessa said. But she said it like a question.

"Maybe not."

"What would you have done?" Elan asked me.

I hesitated. Our presence in the grove had awakened a horde of cicadas; they were screaming in a circle all around us, the sound rising and falling.

"I don't think I would have participated in it, then. I think I would have refused to shoot. Because of my own background. Ron Ridenhour, the G.I. who refused to let the incident be covered up, said he'd studied the Holocaust in high school, and he knew that once having heard about the massacre, if he didn't do something, he would be part of the crime. He didn't go to Vietnam to be a Nazi, he said. But notice I said I *think* I would not have participated. I hope that's right. I know there were times I was weak, and sometimes I was filled with hate..."

"What about now?" Elan insisted, and I was going to do

what I'd do in a class, throw it back to her: ask are you avoiding that answer for yourself? But I suddenly realized how important her question was.

"I wouldn't do it. I would try to stop it."

"How can you say that?"

"Because of what I've learned. Because I've learned about what I should do. I think people have to do that. I think people can do that. Otherwise what's the point of teaching? Or writing? Or film-making? It's all to show us what is possible. What we are capable of. The example of darkness and the example of light." I pointed at the Israeli director. Sitting at an ice-cream kiosk in Hue a few days before, Judd had broken down, recounting a story of how, a combat surgeon on the Golan Heights during the 1973 war, he had found two severely wounded Syrian soldiers next to their tank, which had been hit, and had been forced by his commander at gun point to abandon them to die. It was the first time he had spoken directly about his experience, and what he chose to speak of, what made him weep, what had so clearly wounded him so deeply was that account of a moral failure.

"That's why we're here," I said. "There's no point otherwise."

\*\*\*

The mis-named place now and forever called My Lai was obscene with normalcy. It was a clear, hot day. Palms waved, wind whispered and groaned through the bamboo, grass rustled around the small memorials. "Here the Americans killed 160 people. Here the Americans killed the Ly family." The Vietnamese American students, Jonathan, Pauline and Emily, went from each to each, placing and lighting incense. Thuy and I sat with Truong Thi Le and spoke to her while the other students filmed and asked questions. She is very old now—she was in her forties at the time of the massacre—

and has told her story many times. It was a story I knew. Sitting on the grass next to her, though, I became fascinated with her hands. They were a peasant's hands, strong and gnarled; the tips of her fingers calloused and blunted. As she spoke in her soft voice—the Americans came, and before we had given them water and they said thank you, and now they shot us all, they killed all my children—I watched her fingers pluck strands of grass from the earth of that place and weave them into an impossibly small, tight wreath, and unweave it, and then weave it again, looking down at it—not at us, but at the tiny circle in her hands, unwoven and woven again and again, as she knew it had to be.

Afterwards she took us to the ditch. It looked of course like any other irrigation ditch in the countryside there, concrete-lined, clogged with lily and lotus pads. At one point during the massacre, after Lt. Calley, in charge of the platoon that did much of the killing, had ordered the villagers into this ditch, and had his men shoot and machine-gun them, joining them as they fired into the mass of unresisting flesh—a small child had tried to crawl away, and he'd shot it, picked up the body, threw it in. I squatted and stared into its murky water. I wanted it to be filled with blood. I hated its normalcy, the quiet beauty of water, the soft breeze breaking the heat, its silent comment that this place is like all other places.

Truong Thi Le took the students to the edge, to the place her family was slaughtered. She acted out for them how it had happened. Her husband. Her children. Bang, bang, she said. She had been shot in the head, but the bullet had just grazed her scalp, left for dead under a pile of dead. She parted her hair, with her strong peasant's fingers, and showed us her wound.

\*\*\*

We needed a break. The day after My Lai, we relaxed in Hoi An, some twenty kilometers down the coast from Marble Mountain. The UN has declared the town a cultural preserve, and though there are few modern buildings, the town doesn't have any of the dead sterility connoted by the term "preserve"; its blend of Chinese, Vietnamese and French architecture; its pleasant streets and cafes and Chinese temples remind one of the old sections of Hanoi, on a smaller scale. In fact, the town was used to film parts of *The Quiet American* that were set in Saigon in the 1950s, including the bridge where Pyle, blood on his shoes, "impregnably armored by his good intentions and his ignorance," was killed. It's my son's favorite town in Vietnam, and he was looking forward to showing it to me. The year before, he had fallen in love with Vietnam, in this place, when he'd been walking by an alley, and had suddenly and literally been pulled into a wedding celebration, wined, dined, embraced, sung to, treated like a long lost member of the family.

Hoi An is a port and has always been known for its merchants. The town looked prosperous, filled with arts and crafts shops, sidewalk restaurants and cafes, and get-a-suit-in-one-day tailor shops. The war seemed to occupy only two small rooms: they were upstairs in an old brick building near a covered Japanese bridge, its one end occupied by an altar and statues honoring monkeys, the other with an altar and statues of two dogs. The family Labrador that Adam had grown up with had died that year, so we lit some incense at the dog statues and walked up the stairs to the war. One room had arms, documents and pictures from the anti-French war; the other from the American war. A painting on the wall depicted the capture of some poor G.I. on the beach near Marble Mountain; two women were driving his jeep into the ocean to hide it, others sweeping clear the tire tracks, while a stalwart looking guerilla was leading the American off with a rope around his neck. It was a crude painting, but what made me shudder was the American's boots. They were jungle boots, green and black, and they were depicted very accurately. You could see whoever painted them had known those boots.

O.K, Pop, we're here to get away from the war, Adam reminded me, so we went downstairs and bought some plastic bottles of water from a grizzled man with no right foot. He saw me looking, pointed at it and said, "ARVIN;" he'd been a South Vietnamese soldier. I pressed some money into his palm and walked away.

Before I went back into the hotel, I stepped into a small alley across the street and picked up my laundry. The young woman there seemed to embody the town's energy and mercantile creativity: she ran a photo developing shop, with a little home laundry business on the side. If you brought her your clothes along with the hotel's price list, she would wash and fold everything and have it for you the next afternoon, charging half the price the hotel did for each item, and when she gave it, neatly packaged, back to you, she would laugh, as if inviting you to share her delight at her own ingenuity. It was a merchant's town, and she was funny and charming and open, in the way of the South.

That afternoon, Judd, the Israeli director, and I went out to the beach. The sand was white, the water dark blue streaked with turquoise. I swam for a time, brushing aside clouds of soft, stingless jellyfish, floating on the rocking waves. The beach looked like the stretch near Marble Mountain, though I took photos of that beach when I was based there and what is notable in them are the coiled stretches of barbed wire and the sandbag bunkers, facing the ocean. I'd had my only training in the art of shooting a machine gun from a moving aircraft in that section of the South China Sea, practicing getting a pattern of rounds onto green dye markers, sliding amoebic through the blue ocean: if we hit them they'd explode in geysers of white spray. The trick was to point the end of the barrel below and behind what you wanted to hit; a little more below and a little more behind the higher you went. You braced yourself, legs apart, squinting, fingers touching the butterfly trigger with a butterfly touch.

O.K., you're going to forget the war for now, Judd reminded me. But lying on the beach, I could see clearly the humped silhouettes of the Marble Mountain formation up to our north. I closed my eyes, drank my beer, felt the breeze on my face, listened, as one does, to the sound of waves hitting the beach, shutting one's eyes, letting that noise fill one's head. I felt someone tug at my arm, and when I opened my eyes, the girl from An Tan was standing there, pushing her basket out at my face.

Of course not. There were two girls, and two women, though their clothing was nearly as ragged as that girl's had been. There were no dusty cokes in their baskets, only faux Zippos engraved with unit insignia and cynical grunt epigrams, and wooden bracelets and charms, and plastic water bottles, and tiger balm, and so on. There were swarms of female vendors all over the beach, infiltrating the line of beach chairs like sappers.

"Hi," one said to me. "I'm Lulu."

"Of course you are," I said, and she laughed in a way that startled me. As if she got the joke, as if she was letting me see she got the joke, as if she was saying, I'm not who you think I am.

"Of course I am," she said, and all the girls laughed. I gave in and bought some tiger balm, and then another bottle of water, and another tiger balm, and Judd became deeply involved in a conversation with a girl selling amulets and charms. "If you wear this, it will keep you safe in all your travels," she said, and grinned in that same way: we were all in on the joke, and she was playing her role, and she'd appreciate it greatly if we bought everything but please don't take her role as all she was. "And this, I think, will be good for your wife."

Her English was impeccable. I asked her where she had learned it.

The girls and women settled down around us, the selling over; no other prospects on the beach.

"I'm studying English in high school," she said. She might have been the age of the An Tan girl, perhaps a little older. "I want to go into the tourist industry," she said earnestly. "It will bring us much prosperity here."

"We are already in the tourist industry," Lulu said, and they all laughed. She looked at me. "Why are you crying?" she asked. She gestured at my face, looked to the others, distressed.

I didn't know how to answer her. She was the answer; they all were. I didn't feel responsible for their poverty. They would be all right, these girls and women; like the photoshop-laundress, they glowed with energy and intelligence and charm. They would be all right as Vietnam would be all right. But they had made me fall in love again with Vietnam; not the love I had come to me since I'd been returning, but as I had felt it so many years ago when it had come to me to mean, to be, my own humanity.

"You were in the war," Lulu said, a fact. "The Americans killed my mother and father," she said. Another fact. Not an accusation, simply another fact. "But please don't cry. We can't look back. We don't look back. You're a good man."

She and the other girls had gathered close around my chair, and now they were patting me, as if trying to push down with their hands the sudden swell of grief that had come to me with the memory of how much damage we had done to this place and these people, carving them to fit into our vision, with the desperate ruthlessness of unrequited love. Their hands patted me, calmed me, as I sat and performed the old American trick of seeking comfort from my victims.

# SCENE SIX
The Victors' Unsung Songs:
2000-2001

# THORNS

Binh has found a ruined house built in the French style and now convincingly collapsed. The special effects people light fires here and there for the scene. Air raid sirens blare. Bystanders mill. The Exquisite Do Thi Hai Yen runs into the house as Hoai, a young mother, the wife of Van, the diary-writer, searching for her child. The explosives man, an ex-NVA sapper, touches off one of his charges: plaster showers down. An old man steps out of the shadows next to the building. He is dressed in a war-era People's Army uniform, pressed, his chest bedecked with a row of medals. He stands silently, at rigid attention, staring at the bombed house, tears running down his cheeks, glittering in the flicker of the fires. Extras dressed as wartime fire and rescue people run around him, spraying water at the house. The camera stays on the actress.

Earlier that morning, Binh and I had had *café sua*, the thick coffee drained over condensed milk, in a small café. It was raining outside and the café was small and warm, with stained beige walls, the smell of damp stone and steaming coffee intensified by the weather. We'd wanted to do some work in the sound studio, but the engineer had gotten drunk the night before and didn't show up. Binh took the news calmly, though it meant hours of delay. He seemed to take everything calmly. A Westerner looking at him would see a small, thin, rather nerdy young man. It was a way we had of underestimating the Vietnamese, mistaking bulk for strength, and I knew better. But it occurred to me that I hardly knew him at all.

"What do you think so far?" I asked him. "Is the film living up to your vision?"

He considered the question seriously for a moment. "In some ways," he said finally. "But not in others. I have a picture in my mind—as you say, vision—but it doesn't always work. I liked your scene. The street was good. We had you going this way, under the flag, the woman bringing clothes, the barber, the people moving this way..." He described the action with his hands, small elegant gestures. For a second I had a glimpse of the way he saw: an interflowing of colors and motions, the human components of it working or not working as parts of a composition. There was something comforting in it for me—to be seen not as an individual, but as a thread in a design.

He poured some more coffee into the strainer over my glass, then into his own. "Yes," he said. "You know, I was trained as a painter."

"I didn't know."

"Yes. I studied at the college of art."

"Did you like that?"

"I think it saved my life."

He had grown up, he told me, on the street. His family was very poor. Almost everybody was, in the years after the war, but in their case the poverty was exacerbated because of the stain of having a grandfather who'd been a political prisoner. He'd been teased and bullied in school for the family's lack of political purity, and because he was small and rather weak—there was never much to eat—he was often beaten up. He reacted cinematically, began fighting back, fighting every day in school and after, running with a gang of boys. He learned karate, and fought more. "After a while, that was all I did. I would get up in the morning, and think about who to fight that day."

But he had a talent for drawing. He took what was happening around him and tried to put it on paper, in the lines and colors he saw in his mind. His mother, who had put herself through school and even studied and mastered French and English while working hard labor on a street repair crew, encouraged him, spoke to people, finally got him enrolled in the art college.

"Part of our training," he told me, "was for the students to be sent out into the country, to live for half a year in a small village. To learn how to paint the land, the people. Before then, my eyes only saw narrow spaces." He waved around the café, then out the open door to the tree-lined street, its potholes filled with muddy water. "But it was as if the world opened to me, showed me there were other ways of seeing. It did this to my eyes, but also to my mind and heart, do you understand? Part of why I fought all the time was because we were always so crowded in. In the compound where my family lived, there were forty people who shared one filthy toilet. One stove, one sink. You had to fight to eat, to breath. It made people mad, always mad. Then suddenly I saw so much space and light. It hurt my eyes. And the people acted as open as the space around them. They gave to you, like the fields and trees gave food. We art students could sleep in any house, walk in at any time, and people would feed us, give us a place to sleep, treat us as part of their family. I became calm. I was able to look at my behavior. I stopped fighting."

I shook my head. He asked me what was the matter, and I told him what I'd been thinking. "Listening to you...it just seems so difficult to me, to do what you're trying to do in the film. To get in all the stories. It seems you have to fail."

"Yes, of course," he said serenely. "You know the character of Vinh? We took much of his story from Tran Van Thuy."

"Yes, I know. I like his work very much."

"He filmed so much during the war—he was everywhere. Just one man and a camera. But he tells me each morning he wakes up feeling terrible because he remembers another scene or incident he didn't get on film. Something of someone's bravery, or some horror. He feels great sorrow, he said, like for children who have died. It's like that, isn't it?"

"Yes. I know how he feels." I hesitated. "You know, that's one thing I wanted to talk to you about with the film. You have these five stories, these five guys, but only one dies. I don't think that's very realistic. These guys are in the war for ten years. I think you need to show more of the casualties in their unit. I remember reading about Bao Ninh's unit—out of five hundred men who went South, only ten survived."

"I agree. We will be doing some more sequences, to show the dead on both sides. It's a little delicate—Vietnamese war movies don't show our dead. But you're right." He lit a cigarette. "We need to do it."

The café where we were sitting was on a wide street that cut through town, to the Opera House and the Lake of the Returned Sword, and as I looked up it now I remembered how it had looked last April when the 25th anniversary of the end of the war was celebrated—the day on which the nearly final scenes of the movie were supposed to take place. Red flags with yellow stars flew everywhere, banners embroidered with slogans were hung above intersections, colorful posters of Ho Chi Minh leading groups of workers, peasants, doctors and intellectuals decorated huge billboards, larger than life representations, as if they were the Platonic perfections the people marching in the parades on the streets were attempting to emulate. The public buildings had all been scrubbed and the police were in spotless, pressed white uniforms. As if the whole city were in costume. I knew where my mind was taking me. To see it all as a set, implied hollowness, a façade. *Monuments are taxidermy,* George Evans had written. I needed to be careful here, I thought. No one had paid more for victory celebrations than these people, and no one believed more in the necessity and justice of their cause. "You would have had to kill us all to win," a Vietnamese journalist I'd had dinner with had said to me, when I'd told him many people in America had come to believe that we hadn't been allowed to win the war. I believed him. All the Vietnamese I knew here were that way, and I was glad enough that neither the French nor the Americans owned this country.

But the stench of death still leaked out from under the celebration of any victory, and celebrating victory in a civil war in particular had to mean celebrating the death of part of yourself. Though I suppose that could be said about any war. It tended to cast a pall over the parade. In the States, the year before, I'd read several books and articles that had seized on the fakes and exaggerations that came out of the Vietnam war, as I suspect they would come out of any war, to claim there was really very little trauma among American veterans. The idea that men could see death and could kill without damaging their own souls, or even that they should, seemed deranged until I understood it as part of the need to see the cause as noble. Those who fought the fight of the just should sleep the sleep of the just. A subtext whose echo I'd heard in the words of a Vietnamese friend, a People's Army veteran, who told me that Vietnamese veterans had sustained relatively little psychological damage: their belief in national liberation and socialist revolution had armored their spirits. It wasn't an uncommon attitude; I heard it many times here. Though not everyone bought it.

"Of course there are damaged people here. They're everywhere. We won the war, but we lost three million lives," a woman, another friend, said. "Three million bodies and who knows how many minds and souls." She told me of a male cousin who had been in heavy fighting in the South and who now kept digging bunkers and trenches behind his house and hiding in them, then stripping himself naked and running into the streets. "That making yourself naked is a symptom many veterans show," she said. "You hear of this all the time. I don't know why they do it. Maybe to show they have lost everything."

Binh's full name is Nguyen Phan Quang Binh, but the

last, his given name, means "Peace." The woman who told me about the veterans was his mother, Phan Thanh Hao, who also tells this story of his birth, which took place during the American bombing, and who seems unaware, at times, of her own damage, since she doesn't consider herself a veteran. When I returned with the NYU film students in 2004, I asked Hao to take us to some of the areas where she had witnessed the bombing, and she took us to the outskirts of Hanoi, a neighborhood along the Red River, prosperous now, though utterly destroyed one day in 1967 when un-smart bombs from B-52s missed the targeted factory across the road. Hao belonged, as did many teenagers, to a youth volunteer team assigned to go into bombed areas to dig out survivors and bodies. When she and her team went in, there was nothing but rubble and scattered human parts, but digging out one shelter they found a group of perfectly intact bodies, standing bronzed as, in her description, Roman statues. For a year after, she said, she could not eat meat, and the smell of barbecue still calls unbidden images of the rows of bodies and parts of bodies they pulled from that wreckage. Many of the New York students listening to her had been in Manhattan on September 11th, and the shudder of connection they felt in her description had nothing to do with any cheap ironic notion of karmic payback, but with a pure empathy that would have been impossible before that day: an emotion transformative but much too expensive, and looking at them and at her, I thought of Rupert Brooke's phrase: "Blighted eyes."

According to Hao, about 3,000 had died in that neighborhood, a number that also paralleled the New York bombing. But in Hanoi, a bombing was not the event of a single day, and Hao's eyes were blighted many more times. After a raid, the ruins of the buildings around her seemed to be groaning and screaming, a blending of hundreds of cries into what seemed one voice. The house next to hers was hit; she helped dig out the bodies of the family who had lived in it, laid them out on the street. They were covered with so much dust and dirt they looked like part of it: the corpses and the ruined house like a macabre parody of home and family.

Hao's father, a poet and one of the founders of the Writers' Association, had been imprisoned by the authorities for work perceived, for one reason or another, as politically incorrect, and she hated the people who had arrested him, and she hated the Americans, but after a while she found she could hate no one. She was too tired. She didn't have the energy. She understood, even before she could articulate it, that everyone—the party functionary and the cops who had taken away her father, the American pilot who had blown up the house next door, were acting out fates they couldn't control. She loved her country, wounded and burnt and bleeding around her; she loved it because of its wounds, with a depth otherwise impossible. Her father and mother had taught her to love its literature also, and it sustained her; she knew its great poems by heart, including, of course, the nineteenth century poet Nguyen Du's *Tale of Kieu,* the epic poem of a young woman who is forced to sell herself into prostitution in order to save her family, which foreigners found—her father had told her—a strange poem to be considered by so many Vietnamese as their national saga. How could they not understand, she wondered, as she watched so many from her generation sacrifice themselves, go South to the war, to death; she would have gone herself, but was kept back because of her father. She loved her country. She loved the young men who went South, loved them chastely, but with a desire she knew was the other face of death. In her corvee, she met a man who had returned from the war. His eyes haunted her. Of a thousand who had gone, he told her, he had been the only to survive. Afterwards, they had made him a commando, an assassin of enemy spies and agents. Once, he said, he'd even killed an American making love to a Vietnamese girl. He had killed with his hands, he told her, showing them to her. He had been demobilized. But he didn't belong anywhere anymore. One day he was gone; he'd reenlisted, she heard, went back South, soon he was dead. All of the children were going South. A boy she had grown up with, who had brought her little packets of rice and pork after her father's arrest, stood in front of her, his face down, asking her to walk with him before he went into the army. She did. He wanted to tell her something; she could see it; she knew what he wanted to say. But he couldn't speak. As they walked, he twisted first one and then another button from his tunic, so that when he said goodnight, all of his buttons were gone. When his mother told her, a month later, that he'd been killed in War Zone B, she remembered the buttons, and for the first and last time, she wept. She saw the face of everything that had been thrown from the world.

She met and married Nguyen Quang Hien, a man exempted from the war because of a bad arm.

Going out with the road gang, or with the rescue squad, she'd dug with her hands in the rubble of the thousand-year-old capital, pulling out bodies sometimes pulped, flattened, mutilated, sometimes worse, intact and beautiful: an upside-down child, a smile frozen on her face; a family in a bomb shelter, suffocated when the bomb sucked the oxygen out, peaceful as sleepers, their flesh melted into each other, as if configured into the impossible idea of love.

She needed to have a child. It was an urge as strong and involuntary as breathing.

The planes were attacking when she went into labor. It was 1972, Nixon's Christmas bombing, and the shelter being used as a clinic was, of course, crowded with casualties, and the nurses seemed angry at her for coming in with something as mundane as giving birth. Not that she was alone. She lay on a mat on the filthy floor, dust falling on her face as the bombs hit nearby, shock waves feeling as if they were passing into the amniotic fluid itself, and she saw she was in a row of women, all of them who had gone into labor as soon as the bombing started.

She was ten hours, then twelve, then fifteen on that mat: the baby wouldn't come. Finally, without anesthesia, they cut her, widened her to bring out the child, to stop her screams. The nurses cursing her. When they had finished, they could find no way to close her up again, until the nurse punctured her flesh with needles so blunt and bent they looked to her like thorns, and sewed her up with a few dirty pieces of string, laughing to herself.

This was the birth of Binh, who would one day grow up and direct a scene in which a young woman runs into a bombed house to find her child.

They wanted to get it right, Binh and Hanh had told me. They'd wanted, the kids had said to me, to tell the stories the American war movies left out. I wondered if they would also tell the stories the Vietnamese had left out. The other out-takes. They were still there, under the victory celebrations, everywhere, a parade of hunched and weeping wraiths marching within the parade. The movie still seemed to be pulling them from the air around us, the way a decoy, shaped and painted like a duck, pulled real ducks from the sky.

*Out-take: Killing Love*

As they work in the rubble, the dust of the city rises around them like memories of the explosions that had created the very ruins among which they move. It settles into the pores of their skin, claims them. Son feels himself layered with time; he is being absorbed into the capital, back into the nation. He fights the feeling. He cannot yet be allowed to return. Sifting dirt, prying up fallen stones, digging into heaps of smashed concrete, they often find parts. Fishing for their lunch in a canal they are clearing, a girl nets and pulls up a human arm. On another day, Son works through a collapsed wall, into what had been a noodle shop. On the wall, behind a wire that had been fastened corner to corner to hang noodles, is a face. It stares back at him, eyeless. It slides down as he watches, painting a silent red scream on the wall.

Son keeps a catalogue of the parts in his mind. He thinks of it as his body count, a term he had picked up in the South. But his goal isn't to achieve a high count, to let every bit and piece stand for a platoon of Americans, as he has known several political commissars to do. He is collecting enough only to build two bodies. Mr. American Man and Miss Vietnamese Woman. Unfortunately, too often there is nothing recognizable. And he refuses to cheat by counting parts from children, though those are often the most intact. Hoai, another girl on the labor corvée, had once come across a tiny v-shape in the ground—when she dug down, she had found an entire little girl, head down, the v formed by the soles of her two feet.

Son has the man's face now—it is rubbery enough so he can coach it into Western features if he wants. He has three arms, but all were female. Only one leg. A male torso. Male genitals, nesting on top of a segment of bamboo that stuck out of the stone wall stripped all around it. The little pagoda of the penis. He still needs female genitalia, buttocks, feet. He is confident they will turn up.

They take a break at midday, next to the rubble of a small house that had been used as a museum, and from which they have pulled a smashed carving of the Hanoi turtle. He and the other men wear only shorts and sandals; the girls wear black trousers and blue shirts, and scarves around their faces. Both men and women wrap cloth sweatbands around their heads. Hoai unwraps the kerchief from her face, and unconsciously lets her hand wander over her chin, covering it. She had been working in a small factory, making glass medicine vials, when one blew up in her face, and is self-conscious about the scarring. Son feels a need to comfort her, though he wasn't sure why he chose to do so by running his hand down his filthy chest and stomach, drawing attention to the pits and creases and ridges of his own scars.

Hoai looks into his eyes. Her frankness startles him; most women would not raise their eyes in this way. She has a reputation of being chaste but bold: she holds her head up, seems always to be saying: what else can you do to me? He'd known her before he had left for the battlefield, six years before. He'd thought he loved her then. The night he left, he had asked her to walk with him. But had not gotten up the courage to say what he'd wanted. He had left without saying anything to her; he couldn't speak his love. Now he feels nothing.

"Why are you here, elder brother?" she asks.

"I know," he says, believing she understands him. "I shouldn't be. I'm sorry."

She is still staring at him. Maybe she doesn't understand after all.

"Of a thousand, only me," he explains.

Not that it is surprising he is the only survivor. He was good at the killing. Somewhere in Tay Ninh, after most of his battalion had been wiped out, after they'd seen how good he was, he'd been chosen for the Special Unit, trained him for different duties. At times, these were duties that had to be carried out silently. He has very strong hands. Before the war, he'd been studying engineering, but working on construction gangs, tiling roofs, doing plumbing repairs, hauling bricks, as he'd done since he was ten years old. His hands were like pliers. The fingers that squeezed off his wooden buttons, one by one, when he couldn't speak of love, could grip an Adam's apple and crush it like a grape. He could get one hand around the front of a neck and squeeze the breath out of the target within minutes. He had done it that way only once, to a fat Saigon puppet village-chief who he knew was responsible for the capture and torture of one of the female cadre: she'd been torn to pieces by dogs. He wanted the man to know he was dying, wanted it slow.

He would breath into his own nostrils the last breaths of his targets. They weren't always targets that he could hate as easily as the village chief. Their breaths would linger in his own throat; he'd feel them pour down his windpipe, rise up like bile and blood in his mouth. Afterwards, they settled into stones in his stomach and heart, a heaviness that never left him. He carries all of them with him now.

He had been a good shot too, and he preferred that. Preferred the distance. Preferred also that his targets were Americans. Killing Americans was merely a matter of trigonometry. Angles, distances, windage. They had come to his country, not he to theirs. Their faces in his sights were white or black, alien. Their green uniforms, as they poured out of helicopters, made him think of insects. As a combat infantryman he had been in battles, but they were confusing, impersonal: everyone firing as fast as they could, bullets whipping back past his own head, the deafening noise, and finally the inevitable withdrawal when the enemy planes and helicopters came. In his new job he was rarely shot at, at least not until after he'd made his kill, and with each kill he'd at first felt an elation: he was ridding the land of its invader; it was why he had volunteered. He knew some of it was relief that he wasn't doing the other killing. He knew he had to accept both. He was a weapon, to be used as his country wished. He was given missions. He terrified a perimeter at a firebase near Danang, hitting targets through the slits of bunkers. Near Ky Ha one night, he came across a silent bunker, slithered inside, and saw three Americans and three Saigonese soldiers, all sound asleep. He took them one by one, with his knife; in the morning their comrades would find them, be filled with fear. Go home, he told each dead American. He killed a new American consul in Hue with a clean shot through the forehead. He took targets assigned and targets of opportunity. Once, on his way through the jungle to a unit that had requested his services, he came across nine Americans bathing in a stream. Their clothing and equipment were on the bank, with one boy still dressed and on guard, sitting on a rock. He took that one out first, came up behind him with his knife, so the others wouldn't have time to scramble out into the jungle on each side. He lay down prone on the rock, put his AK on full automatic, figuring that when he began firing, he would start with the boy furthest away, and as the rest would run towards him, he'd sweep the line, quickly. The first target rose from the water, frolicking, splashing. Son sighted on the middle of his chest. He was used to seeing the Americans layered in their green uniforms, helmets, flak jackets—it was easy to see them that way as alien, hated invaders—and for a second he was taken aback at the vulnerable flesh: the tan arms, the white, white chest, the blond hairs he could see clearly, one by one, the penis and testicles, shrunken in the cold water. There was only one way to erase the sudden vision, and he squeezed the trigger, carved the flesh out of its sudden humanness, moved the barrel quickly up the line, and then down again, until all of them were bobbing gently in the water, their hair flowing like grass.

The jungle was silent: the normal sound of birdcalls stilled, as if the birds were in shock from the noise of the shooting.

Or more likely, had simply flown away. He remembered an old man he'd met, a bird expert, whose job in the People's Army had been to visit various units coming down the Ho Chi Minh Trail and, staying in the jungle, trill bird calls at them. The birds that would normally be there had fled, or were dead, from the shock of the bombings, the sprayed chemicals, and it was felt the morale of the soldiers would improve if they could hear such songs as they moved South. He should leave now. But this group had seemed isolated, and he had never been able to look at the Americans this closely. He began rummaging through one of the packs. Perhaps it had belonged to the first boy he had killed, the blond. The image of him rising from the water, bleeding back into it came to Son's mind.

He shook his head. In the pack were socks, a green t-shirt, a small diary. He riffled the pages, picturing the English words flying off them, joining the soul of their creator, now a *ma da*, a water ghost. The only other object in the pack was a blue-green carton of cigarettes. It was open, and he extracted a pack, tore its corner, and put the filtered cigarette in his mouth. It felt artificial, alien as these soldiers. He lit it with his own lighter. He was breaking all of his own rules. The smoke was cool, sweet, in his mouth and throat, tasted of mint. He put the carton back in the pack, swung the pack over his shoulder, and got out of there.

Its weight joined the other weight he was carrying all the time by now: the friends he'd seen killed at Tay Ninh, the ones he'd killed, it made no difference, they were all settling into weight, their deadness creeping like ice into his throat, heart and stomach, their heaviness making it hard for him on some days to even move, and he lay or sat in one place, motionless for hours. Tasting them on his lips, mint and tobacco. Others looked at him at such times with awe and admiration at his self-discipline. But he knew that he was dead. He had caught death. He had taken it in him too many times. He was a ghost now, invisible, a wandering soul moving among the living.

One day, about two weeks after he'd killed the bathing

Americans, he met with his commander in a tunnel a few kilometers from the American base at Phu Bai. The entrance was under the lip of the bank of a stream, under a bush. He hated worming his way through the tunnels. Their walls hugged his shoulders and back, pressed in on him: if he lost his power of motion here, he would be absorbed into the earth. He was dead and now buried. The tunnel opened into an earthen bubble, large enough for four people, high enough to sit upright, but not stand. His commander was sitting behind a plank table, candlelight flickering on his face, his eye sockets black as if set in a skull. The face kept changing as Son watched: an elderly woman in Phan Thiet, the village chief, the smile that had lit the face of the naked American just before Son took it away.

"Are you alright, Son?"

"Yes, commander."

"Good." He ran a bony finger along the map spread on the plank table, tapping. "The American Marines in this area have been running what they call a Combined Action Company. Do you know what that is?"

"Yes, commander." It was a strategy only the American Marines had adopted: the Combined Action Companies were made up of men taught Vietnamese and village customs; they would work with the villagers, help build schools and set up clinics, train a village militia, what the puppet army called Regional Forces. He knew the strategy had been successful enough to worry the high command, so much so that prices had been put on the head of CAC Marines.

The commander was showing him the locations of the American units. He had another list that contained their names and ranks. He showed it to Son, but then folded it up and put it into the ammunition box under the table. "Such information doesn't really affect your mission," he said.

Son nodded. He wasn't surprised at the amount of intelligence the commander had. They would have their own people in the villages, of course. And the tunnel he was in was part of a network that extended right under their base:

there was a listening post under their headquarters. The Americans were careless with their radio traffic as well: they apparently assumed that the liberation forces were too unsophisticated to monitor transmissions, that they had no one who could understand English.

"Their fucking Sa-lems," the commander said.

"Commander?"

He pulled out a pack of cigarettes, showed it to Son. It was the same kind of cigarettes he had taken from the boy he'd killed in the stream.

"Do you know what this is?" the commander demanded.

"Yes, of course."

"No, you don't. This is the counter-revolution. This is what the Americans have instead of religion. The new missionaries and the new opium of the people. It tastes so new, our peasants say. For this the revolution is betrayed."

By the next day, Son had set himself up in a banyan tree, in a grove a few kilometers outside the perimeter of one CAC squad assigned to a small hamlet near Phu Bai. He was doing an initial assessment, looking for fire points, targets of opportunity, when he was startled to hear the rustle of bushes, the sound of whispers. A thrill of fear went through him like electricity running in his veins. He'd never been caught unawares like this. He remained perfectly still. He realized he was enjoying the fear. It was the first emotion he had felt in months. Also, he was in control now. His targets were coming to him.

Looking down, he saw an American and a young Vietnamese woman walking into the grove. The American wore green fatigue trousers and a green t-shirt, and had an M-16 slung casually over his shoulder. One sleeve of the t-shirt was rolled, seam folded up to the man's shoulder; the formed pocket holding a blue-green pack of cigarettes. Otherwise, the American was bareheaded, and wore Ho Chi Minh rubber sandals, made from tires. The Vietnamese woman didn't look like a village girl. She was dressed, for one thing, in an ao dai, and her skin was too fair, her hands smooth. One of her hands was being held by the American.

He remained perfectly still. The two sat, legs crossed as if in a meditation posture, staring at each other. Then they reached out and traced each other's faces with their fingertips. He watched the fingers of the American brush the young woman's closed eyelids.

*Anh yeu em,* he heard the American say. I love you.

*Em yeu anh,* the woman said. I love you. And your accent is much better.

I had a good teacher, the American said. I missed you. I've been feeling so crazy, like I'm losing myself, Phuong. I need.

The woman's mouth tightened. Show me, she said.

Son looked away, to the sky, through the branches. He heard them below. When he looked again, they had laid their clothing on the ground and were embracing, their flesh merging, the naked skin of the American filling him with weight. Their soft moans rose to him, like the cries of the wounded he had heard so often. He couldn't move. He knew if he shot from here, he'd be dead: he was too close to the American positions in the hamlet. But he knew his paralysis was more than that. He was dead, and it suddenly seemed that they were showing him how he could be alive. All he had to do was remain silent. All he had to do was remain still. If he let them live, he would be alive. It was that simple. He put the AK firmly into the fork of a branch. Then, silently, with the economy of motion he had practiced on so many occasions, he slid down the trunk of the tree, on the opposite side from the lovers. When he came around to their side, he had his knife in his hand. He pulled the American's head up by the hair and slit the carotid swiftly. The girl was looking at him with heavy-lidded eyes, and passed uncomprehending into death as he pushed the point of his knife down and into and through her throat, until he felt it slide into the earth upon which she had lain with the American. It had been easy, he found, to kill love.

# HOUSE RULES

The hotel room on Le Van Huu Street was large, clean, and high-ceilinged, in the old French style. It had yellow walls, heavy black teak furniture, ornately carved into dragons and yin/yang symbols; a ceiling fan, a huge armoire, and the largest bed in Hanoi. On the wall near the bed a laminated list of rules was posted: two parallel columns, like the tablets of the ten commandments: one in Vietnamese, the other in what Phan Thanh Hao called Vietglish. *Rule number 7: Animals, weapons, explosions, inflammable materials, and disgusting badly smelt things are not allowed in the room.*

There were double doors that opened to a balcony overlooking the street. I went out and stood looking down at the tops of purple-flowered bougainvillea trees, at the street pulsing with colors and light and motion fragmented through their laced canopies. Le Van Huu was lined with *pho*, noodle soup stalls, and customers hunkered over steaming bowls set around the communal tables, their low blue plastic stools blocking the narrow sidewalks. Nearby, street barbers were clipping the heads of men perched on folding chairs, while next to them women stacked bamboo cages stuffed with miserable chickens, their bead eyes darting frantically, as if all the panicky motion their confined bodies were calling for had shot into them. The intersection swarmed with motor scooters, bicycles, and cyclos, their horns blaring like the sonar emissions of bats, swerving around each other in near collisions, forming, I sensed, a pattern, glimpsed but not understood; when I finally understood it, I would belong here.

Some of the café people and noodle soup vendors were staring up at me and I smiled and nodded at them over-enthusiastically.

I drank my coffee and looked down at the corner. It was crowded with clusters of cone-hatted women, in from the countryside, squatting behind heaps of vegetables and flowers that blazed in reds and yellows against the chipped and muddy pastels of the buildings, or became muted and blurred in the daily rains. "Hello, hello," they called to me, and I waved to them, to the whole scene, feeling suddenly a kind of stupid happiness at simply being here, as if the people on the street going busily about their lives were a counter-parade to the invisible procession of dead and damaged I'd sensed here after the anniversary celebrations, the hidden parade, all the explosions, the inflammable material and disgusting badly-smelt things that weren't allowed in the room. I stood on the balcony for a time, until I became once again aware of a different persona standing with me, one I'd call John: a younger self peering at me over the rim of a foxhole, staring in complete disbelief at the middle-aged man he'd become, at ease in the enemy capital.

There was a knock on the door. When I opened it, Ho Anh Thai strode in and began examining the room critically. I pointed to the blanket on the bed; it was imprinted with pictures of little angels and the repeated phrase: "I love you/ I love you/I love you: Be My Little Angle." I explained the difference in the spelling. "Mr. American Man," he said laughing, and we embraced. I looked behind him, but he was alone; I'd expected Khue to come with him.

"Her daughter is taking the high school finals; your younger sister"—he used the Vietnamese form of address—"is helping her study."

I nodded. I was disappointed, but knew how devoted she was to Phuoc. In our letters and conversations we often spoke about our kids: her daughter was seventeen, my son a few years older. We were both frantically overprotective parents; we both understood why.

I showed Thai Rule 7. He laughed. "Can you manage?"

"It's a restriction I have to live with." I looked at him. "How about you?"

He smiled sourly and said nothing. He was fiercely nonconformist and daring in his writing, and he cared only for writing. But he knew that to live in the room, he had to know and abide by the rules—and he knew the rules were more complex and flexible than they seemed. Things could be done with them. They were never one thing.

"Mr. American Man," he said again.

We both grinned. One of the times I'd come to Hanoi, he'd arranged for me to stay in another mini-hotel near the Lake of the Restored Sword where none of the staff spoke English: I was the only Western guest, and referred to by that name. *Chao ong, Hello, hello, Mister American Man.* He and Khue had adopted it since; his emails addressed to MAM.

"Middle-Aged Man," I said. "You know what else? I remembered this the last time I got an email from you— Military Age Male. It's what we used to call the Vietnamese we suspected could be Viet Cong."

"How fitting. You've become VC, yes?"

"I've been so accused."

"Yes. But now you're Mister Movie Star. Why have they called you back—I thought the film was finished."

"Apparently not. They want to rewrite parts of the script, reshoot some scenes."

After my work on the film had been finished last August, I'd gone home, thinking then that the filming was to be wrapped up in a few months. But now—in May—I'd gotten another email from Binh and Hanh asking me to return: there were some problems.

He laughed. "Anyway I'm glad we're getting a chance to see you. But I think some people will be glad there's trouble."

He named a man we both knew. "Instead of *Song of the Stork,* he calls it *Song of Your Cock.*"

"Why the hostility?"

"Oh, some think they're too ambitious. Others because it's something new, and they weren't supposed to succeed. Others because the war is something they don't think they have a right to touch."

"Bullshit; they're good kids." I began rummaging in my bag. "I have a few presents for you and your family. The DVD is for you. This is for your brother and sister-in-law and the kids."

"*Sunshine,*" he read the title of the DVD. "What's this about?"

"I think you'll like it." I handed him the large teddy bear that had drawn stares in customs. "This is for your son."

He looked at the purse I'd brought his niece. "She'll like this," he said, ignoring the bear.

Another thing that was not allowed in the room. It was very Vietnamese. If you don't want to reply, don't, and people will understand and not press. So I didn't. I was somewhat worried about him though. I knew that Thai and his wife were separated, but that was all I knew. We were close, closer I think than he was with many of his Vietnamese friends because he could say things to me, as a foreigner, he'd feel more restricted about with them. Not necessarily about politics, but other subjects that the complex web of social and familial relationships would make difficult. But he wrapped whatever was happening in his marital life tightly inside himself. Yet he seemed happy, at least as happy as writers get, and particularly happy with the family life he did have. I remembered how good it was visiting him at his house, with his brother and sister-in-law: a unit of people that seamlessly, humorously, lovingly fit with each other— his niece taking my hand and not letting it go, with an ease that seemed to mark the complete security they felt with each other, extended to someone accepted by one of their own. It was a lovely enfolding, but, as with everything else in Vietnam, it was more than that.

When Thai had come to visit me in the rural area where I live, he couldn't understand how people could live in houses set so far from each other. Thai, the fiercely independent writer who knew how to stretch the rules, knew also that without being fibered to some defining knot of family, he might be left unraveled, set as adrift as a wandering spirit, the ghost most Vietnamese, secured as they were into a holding skein of relationships, feared most to become. Not an unusual need, but this was more. This was a house rule, rooted in the turbulence of history and war. For those of the generation before Thai's, those middle-aged men and women, Military Age Males and Females who had come back from the battlefields, the cultural imperatives of marriage and children had been reinforced almost to hysteria by the decimation of their generation. People came back from the war hungry for normalcy and continuation: to have a family, to have a child, to affirm survival, to create the evidence around themselves that a future was possible. That they had defeated death. You married whom you could. You married someone you were attracted to, who was socially suitable, who could give you a child, who was available. Who was alive. Love was something else. Love was something you found later, maybe, not something you waited for. If you did find it after you'd created your place in the world, you took it, you enjoyed it, you romanticized it—and you kept it separate from the reality and the stability of your family. There was *tinh*—passion, emotionalism, spontaneity, love, and there was *nghia*—duty, adherence to unwritten social norms. It wasn't an oppositional relationship; you accepted both. Yin lived with yang. You shared the cold flesh of the dead whenever you shared the warm flesh of a new lover. You entered the relationship with the mutual recognition that opportunities for earthly joy should not be passed over lightly…but also that such love could be as short as a burst of machine-gun fire, or the blast of a bomb, and so best kept temporary, compartmentalized, not to be trusted unless tied somehow, by blood or economic or social necessity or social approval, to a lack of choice that could ultimately kill it. Nothing was ever only one thing. Everything contained its own reverse. You did what you had to so that the center would hold. You created whatever center you could create and clung to it.

As my friend Thai had done, in his conformist/ nonconformist way, and when once he told me a story about a girl he had known, I found myself thinking about what the story told me about him. The girl had been one of the children he'd been evacuated with when he was a kid, taken from Hanoi to a small, supposedly safe village in the country during the American bombing. The girl's parents had come to see her, and were killed when an American plane bombed the village. The girl disappeared; no one could find her. Years later, Thai ran into her in Hanoi, and found that she had been, in essence, adopted by—or had adopted herself—a mentally impaired veteran who had wandered into the village, and had found her after the bombing and taken her to Hanoi. Each had found someone to take care of. She had created a family that parodied the family she'd lost, but at least she had it. She had done what she could. You did what you could. Like the stork, if you knew you were to be killed and cooked, you tried to turn the bad karma into something good: you made sure that at least the water would be clean.

I thought about the way Thai's choice to tell the girl's story reflected his own, mirroring, need for a center, a place in the order of things; I thought about the way the meaning of the film's title somehow became clear to me only after that story placed me into the perception of someone who would understand its framing fable. It was that shift which allowed the connection, just as reading the Vietnamese stories Khue and Thai had sent me over the last ten years let me feel the same way I had when I'd first looked at Khue's face and saw it as if it were emerging from jungle and in that light-bathed moment I'd known how she would have seen me during the war. And found I could mourn whatever had been subtracted in me that would have once allowed me to kill her. *I want to make you see*, Conrad had said. *So that it should be harder to kill*, those of us who wrote about that war could add, should add. *So that killing would be suicide*, we should add; it was what we'd been given to do. I could be me and not me. Not me and yet me. I could not be Thai or Khue. It was not allowed. Or I could. I could not be the girl in Thai's story. Or I could, if I could find what threaded me to her, if I could see, just a little, through the eyes that blessing would give me.

"So tell me more about the film," Thai said.

*Out-take: Homecomings*

Even though she is only six, the girl, Lanh, knows from the way the country suddenly opens and changes when the train takes them over the Long Bien Bridge and out of Hanoi, that her eyes have changed the way they see. Before this she has fit into a flow of people and space that seemed fluid but was really fixed, held as the river was by two banks. Her eyes would, could, wander only so far before her vision was stopped and held by buildings, leaning into each other as if they were tired. The sky itself, whenever she brought her head back on her neck to stare at it, was like the river, banked by two jagged rows of tiled roofs. Every morning at the same time she would watch the twin Ngo brothers on the iron balcony across the street, pouring water they'd ladle from a large tin cistern over their heads and chests. She walked to school down a street lined with bougainvillea trees, her plastic knapsack on her back, wearing her red scarf and red shorts. She said good morning auntie, to Auntie Lam, selling shoelaces and sometimes bananas and lychees on the corner. Everything and everyone was known and named. She was younger sister and daughter and there were older sister and uncles and aunts and fathers, and each was as fastened to a name and a house and a particular combination of shapes, colors, tastes and smells, a quality of filtering, sparkling dust. To her. Passing Hoan Kiem Lake early in the morning, the old men and women doing tai chi by the shore, moving as if they were under the waves, the lovers sitting on the benches, she would look not at the Tortoise Pagoda, but for the Turtle itself, the divine Tortoise that her father had told her had taken back the magical sword of the Emperor Le Loi after he had used it to drive out the Chinese invaders. She would stare and stare, learning how to slide her sight under the sparkle that played on the water like the glittering scales of armor, until she could make out its giant dark form, gliding just under the surface of the lake, and she'd see its scaly head, draped with moss and the occasional floating scraps of trash, barely break through, its cold eyes staring at her. Good morning, grandfather, she would say, and the Tortoise would blink at her, the transparent carapaces of its lids slightly magnifying its liquid gaze.

When the first bombs fell, she huddled in the shelter with the others. She felt the ground rock and shudder and the shudder moved into her skin and didn't stop. Dust puffed from the walls and ceilings with each blast. A network of fissures drew itself on the wall, illuminated by the flickering kerosene lamp; the splash of its light seemed to further elongate the cracks. Those inside held onto to each other, as if they thought their flesh more solid than the dissolving concrete. It wasn't. After that, some adults became enormous, as big as gods. Others became children, frolicking or whining in the ruins. She saw patients tending doctors in a collapsed hospital. In school one day, she saw her teacher weep like a child, and wet his pants, while the custodian became the Emperor Tran Hung Dao defeating the Mongols, protecting his subjects, telling them where to sit and how to move and act. Things fell apart.

You must go, my darling, her mother whispered to her. "But who will say good morning to the Tortoise?" she had demanded. Her mother and father glanced at each other, and then her father smiled grimly. "Maybe he'll decide to restore the sword to us," he said. "It seems like it would be a good time." He squatted down, took her shoulders in his large, callused hands. "Lanh," he said, "it's time you grew up. You have to take care of yourself. We'll come and visit just as soon as we can," he said.

On the train, moving out of the city, she sees, for the first time, the open expanses of rice fields, and all she had seen and heard over the last days comes together into a knot she feels open behind her forehead and flow out into the air. The world can be this, or it can be that. The revelation frightens her more than the sudden scream of the airplane, the whistle and explosion of the falling bombs—these have grown normal and expected. The train screeches to a stop and she is told to run off with the others into a rice field. She lays on a dike, looking back to the city. As she watches, the city turns into a field of gigantic roses and then disappears.

The space and light around the village confuses and disorients her. She stands outside her new parents' house and sees nothing but the green of the rice fields, a single areca tree, the river, its water yellow with floating pollen, and then the black jagged line of mountains like dragon's teeth biting the sky. But, never mind dragons, the house is behind her, its thatched roof covered with drying sugar cane leaves, and her mat is in a room hung with fruit and corn ears, thick with the salty smell of nuoc mam, held in the cool earthen jars around her. She soon calls Cao and Duc mother and father, and Kim elder sister, and Thang, until he goes South to the war, elder brother, and in the morning Cao smiles at her with lacquered teeth as she wraps her hair in a bun, and gives Lanh a hot glass of soybean milk, full of sugar.

She and the other boys and girls from Hanoi can go into any of the houses, and the aunts and uncles will smile at them and give them sugar cane, or, if it is meal time, a plate filled with whatever they were eating, and often give the children bigger portions than their own. Instead of the cramped, dark smelly toilet she had shared with the other families in her housing unit, now she goes to the fields, and squats, feels the breeze across her backside. The world has reformed, and she knows now it can, that more than one shape is possible. But it no longer disturbs her. She goes to classes in a pagoda built around a sloping brick courtyard. Teacher Chinh is a kindly man, a Hanoian like them, he tells the evacuee children, as he points to his heart with tobacco-stained fingers. One day, she recites the opening lines of Kim Van Kieu by memory to him—

she doesn't understand them, but her father had taught them to her, and she will often, at night, on her mat, repeat them, the lines becoming companions for her, as much as the Tortoise had been:

> *A hundred years—in this life span on earth*
> *How apt to clash, talent and destiny!*
> *Human fortunes change even as nature shifts—*
> *The sea now rolls where mulberry fields grew.*
> *One watches things that make one sick at heart.*
> *This is the law: no gain without a loss,*
> *And Heaven hurts fair women for sheer spite.*

Teacher Chinh listens to her and then turns away, and she sees two tears fall from his black eyes, glisten on his cheek. It makes her nearly cry herself, from happiness and pride.

Then Mad Tinh appears. Her friend Thai, one of the other Hanoi children, is at the train station: later he describes Tinh's arrival to her. The train had stopped and then left and when Thai looked, Tinh was standing, heels together, hands pressed to the seams of his ragged, filthy trousers. Thai had not seen him get off the train. It was as if he and the train had arrived on parallel tracks, one pair invisible to anyone but Tinh. The man was dressed in the rags and tatters of a soldier's uniform, a battered pith helmet with a faded red star worn backwards on his head, his bare feet shoed in dirt.

Tinh walks into the village and then stands for a long time in front of the house of a woman named Hai Mat, whose husband Cuong, like most of the husbands, has gone to the war. Two lines of drool fall from the corners of his mouth. Hai Mat comes out, sighs, and talks quietly to him. Then he goes to another house, stands and stares, and another, and another. Some of the villagers come out and look at him, but no one says anything. A woman presses a bowl of rice, sardines and nuoc mam in his hand, and he puts it on the ground and laps from it like a dog. The children laugh, and their parents let them, but say nothing to Tinh. When he comes to Lanh's house, she is squatting outside, playing with a beetle she has attached to a string and is letting buzz in circles around her head. Tinh's shadow falls on her. She looks up, into eyes that are black wells. They seems to be drawing her in, pulling apart the seams of the day around her, one by one. She screams and runs inside. Through the door, she sees Tinh squat and poke at the beetle, then pick it up and eat it. "Buzz, buzz," he says, and pulled off his rags and rolls naked in the dust, then sits in it, patting it on his body as if he were bathing. Lanh screams and screams.

Mother Cao picks her up and holds her. "It's all right, little one. What we send to the war sometimes comes back to us."

He was, some of the village children whisper to her later, a famous American-fighter. But his soul has been cut from his body and now wanders, lost. If he stays here, where his umbilical cord is buried, the villagers say, perhaps it would find him.

Mad Tinh becomes part of the village, the landscape. People feed him, and sometimes he wanders off for days, but he always returns. Lanh can't accept him, can't weave him into her new vision. He is the bomb falling on the street, the bridge: he tears the world apart again. She cries or screams whenever she sees him, runs away as fast as she can.

At harvest time, the fields become a patchwork of green and gold, and she learns how to walk in a line with the women and other girls and grab two clusters of rice stalk with one hand and cut them off close to the ground with the scythe in one swift, neat motion, to leave only a short, jagged stubble. The cool mud squishes up between her toes, releases a rich, pungent odor. She is coming back from the fields one day— Cao, to her delight, had put her on the back of the water buffalo—when she sees her Hanoi mother and father, standing in front of Cao's house, her father wearing a uniform like Mr. Tinh's, though not as ragged, leaning on a wooden crutch. One of the legs of his trousers has been pinned up, and her eyes search the ground frantically for the foot that would fill him in, allow him to form to her memory of him. For a moment she stands, confused, shapes forming, shattering, reforming in her mind.

But only for a moment, and then she runs to them, crying, feels their arms embrace her. Behind her, the other Hanoi children stand silently, their eyes shining with envy and joy. "Lanh, come bathe with us," Thai calls out, suddenly, his voice strained.

"Go bathe with the others, daughter," Cao says. "Wash the mud off, then come home and we'll all eat."

Her mother kisses her, all over her face, her eyelids. "Go ahead, Lanh. We'll help Mrs. Cao."

She runs off with the others, her heart singing, oblivious to the glum faces of the Hanoi children. They and the village children have gradually coalesced, formed groups and alliances that had nothing to do with where one or the other comes from, only age, sex, personalities, likes and dislikes. But the appearance of these two parents from the city suddenly splits them into their original groups, and while the village children laugh and sing, the Hanoians remain silent. Lanh suddenly feels she is in neither group. When they strip off their clothing and jump into the river, she is aware, for the first time, of her nakedness, and hides herself behind a curtain of reeds. A picture comes into her mind: Tinh bathing in dust outside her house. She shudders.

At that moment, a huge noise booms all around her, shaking the reeds, slapping hot air down on her back and head. All of the children freeze, their silence like the wake of the noise. They have all heard it before. Now it has followed them here. A second later she sees something she hasn't seen since the day she'd left Hanoi: a silver jet streaking across the sky, and then swooping down towards the village.

The pilot has no more targets. He's expended his load on the Red River bridge, as he'd done last week, seeing, in his sights, the patchwork repairs jerry-rigged since his last visit. We bomb it, they build it back, he thinks. Coming back time and again to this stretch of river, leaving friends who are literally gone in a flash, erased, he's had the vision of the arched back of a huge black turtle, breaking the waves: he returns here over and over to endlessly blow-up an endlessly regenerating beast.

But the SAMs had been worse this time: he had to dive and dodge frantically, and one missile streaked by so close he could literally read the numbers on its fuselage. Escape and Evade. Then he realized he had been cut off from his wing man and the rest of the squadron. The plan, in such circumstances, was to wheel north and west, and then circle back around, come up over the heavier coastal defenses from behind. Which is what he is doing, when he realizes he still has a bomb hung up on his right wing. He looks below for a TO, Target of Opportunity. For a few seconds—he is burning gas, hauling ass—he sees nothing but paddies, a green and gold patchwork, and then, in the middle of it, the island of a village. Good enough. He dives in close, sights, releases. Feels, as always, the bomb leaving not the plane but his own body: a giddy rush, a sudden lightness. The explosion blooming like a rose behind him as he heads home.

The children scream and run back toward the village.

There was only one bomb and it had fallen on only one house. The children, still dripping wet, stand silently as the adults form a bucket brigade from the well and paddies, futilely throw water on the house. The sugar cane leaves on the roof send a thick sweet smell into the air. An earthen jar filled with fish sauce suddenly explodes, splattering sauce like blood. The heat of the flames dries the water on the bodies of the children.

It isn't until much later, after the structure is nothing but ashes, and they are sifting through for the bones of Cao and Duc and the visitors from Hanoi, that Teacher Chinh looks over at the crowd of children, still standing, shivering, for Lanh. She is gone. He asks the other children if they have seen her. They look at each other as if waking from a dream.

Lanh is in a tunnel that presses in on all sides and only leaves her one direction to go, and she takes it. It is a gray tunnel, and soft as ash, but an ash that will not yield or dissolve. Instead it turns rubbery and stubborn when she would touch it. She knows to follow the tunnel. At its end, she steps out into the light and the railroad station is in front of her. This is where she had disembarked when she'd come from Hanoi, and it is where her parents must have come also. It isn't much of a station: really just a woven palm-frond awning, and some jars of water on the hard-packed earth. If she can follow the tunnel it will take her back not in space but in time to before her trip, before her parents' trip. The black bombs will tumble upwards, in reverse, into the bellies of the planes. In the village, sows and goats give birth, and a woman also, and when she thinks of the bombs, she sees them as infants, sucked backwards into the birth canal, where they would curl and stay.

She feels a hand on her shoulder, and when she looks up, she isn't surprised to see Crazy Tinh. The hand is hard and scarred, the yellow nails long and pointed. He doesn't frighten her. His eyes, under the scabs and crust surrounding them; the eyes she has always been afraid to look into, are mirrors of her own pain. As soon as she looks into them, she becomes aware of that pain, and she begins to howl. Crazy Tinh pats her shoulder, and then embraces her, holding her against him, rocking. She breathes in a smell of stale sweat and blood and finds it comforting; the odors of a living body. He takes off his shirt and puts it on her: it is ragged, but comes down to her ankles His bare chest is streaked with filth and crisscrossed with the raised welts and puckered craters of old scars. As they stand, a train pulls up: it is the weekly train to Hanoi. The conductor looks at Tinh and the girl, nods, helps them up. Crazy Tinh sometimes rides back and forth: the crews know him, and his past, and gave him free passage. He sits Lanh next to him on the hard wooden bench.

On the way, one of the train crew finds some black trousers and a singlet for Lanh, and gives Tinh his shirt. He nods gravely, like a father. But in Hanoi, he seems bewildered, a child again. Lanh takes his hand and leads him through the streets near the railroad station. It is dark, and no one is out except beggars and the railroad prostitutes. Lanh stops before two girls standing in front of an alley and holds out her hand. Crazy Tinh looks at her and follows suit. The girls laugh, tell them to go away. They don't move. The two girls look at them, and one shudders. "That you daddy, younger sister? Maybe mine look like that now too." She presses a few *dong* into Lanh's hand. "Get the hell out of here now, younger sister," the other said.

"Home," Lanh says. She shakes her head.

"Home," Crazy Tinh says.

"You're both nuts," the other girl says uneasily. "Leave 'em. Let's get the hell out of here, us." She looks around nervously. Lately the people's militia have been sweeping the area near the station, picking up people for the labor corvées.

The other girl shakes her head. "What about Uncle Trung's?" she says.

"I don't have fucking time."

"Fucking time is all we got. Stay here, you want."

Trung, a beggar both girls have used as a shill, had been found dead on the street the day before. He had picked up an un-detonated American CBU that had remembered its function as soon as it was in his sack. The girl—her name is Thuy, though she no longer uses it—leads Lanh and Tinh back over the tracks, through rows of ramshackle tin sheds, a maze of twisted metal, bamboo frameworks splintered like broken fingers, jagged pieces of smashed concrete, all of it set haphazardly into what seems a sea of black ash. A piece of tin is propped up by bamboo poles set in the shadows of a narrow alley, against a ruined brick wall, jute sacking piled on the ground under the tin. Thuy points.

"Home," she says.

Lanh nods. She takes Tinh's hand and leads him to it, then makes him sit on the sacking. She sits next to him and stares out at the junkheap visible past the mouth of the alley.

Thuy shakes her head and leaves.

When she is gone, Lanh takes some of the jute sacking and drapes it down over the sides of the little lean-to. She tells Tinh to stay, and makes him lie down, covers him with more sacking. She had thought to look for her parents, but she understands now they are gone. While he sleeps, she goes out and begs more money, steals a little bowl from a pho restaurant near the station, and then does what she had seen the Buddhist monks do: holds it in front of her, on the sidewalks, in front of several cafes. People put dong in, and sometimes rice and a little fish. That night, when the air-raid siren goes off, and the tracers begin flying up at the American bombers, flashes and flares brilliantly, if briefly, illuminating the night, Crazy Tinh begins trembling and silently crying, tears and drool running down his face. Using the sleeves of her new blouse, she wipes his eyes and nose and mouth, and holding him against her, under the noise of the bombs, she begins to tell him about a giant tortoise that lives in the lake. She knows now that what she had seen, when she was a little child, were just floating bits of garbage and debris, tangled together into a suggestive shape by duckweed. But it doesn't matter. All that matters is to keep standing the flimsy walls she has built around the two of them.

# SCENE SEVEN
## An Exaggerated Spiritual Crisis:
## 2001

# THE TWENTY-FIFTH PLATOON

We drive about forty clicks north of Hanoi, past a green and gold patchwork of rice fields, and up into the mountains. Our small convoy turns off the highway at a dirt road that winds up to the site, the same area where we'd filmed last August: rice and corn fields, a red-mudded flat area, some stone and thatched houses, all held between jungled hills that stand lushly green against large, jagged limestone peaks. It is raining and a white mist tendrils around the black slopes, the green and black and red melting, a composition in a war photo.

Since the second filming began, another foreign company has been given permission to film in Vietnam, a joint Australian-American production of *The Quiet American*. The film will star Michael Caine, as Greene's cynical British journalist Fowler, fighting the well-intentioned and hence deadly American Pyle for the right to exploit Vietnam, (as metaphorically embodied in the usual mysterious and emotionless oriental enigma Phuong) for their own ends. In fact, Phoung is being played by the Exquisite Hai Yen, who has finished her work on *Stork*. Their production dwarfs ours, in personnel, in money, in equipment. They even used some of the sites we had used previously, including the one where we are filming today. Looking at it, I see a ditch lined with rows of sandbags and concertina wire, the red mud around it pocked with holes, some of the foliage blackened. Ammo boxes, c-ration cans, some helmets and other equipment lay scattered everywhere. The word that comes to me is "waste." They had taken the hill. They owned the day. We'd be the small guerilla unit, peering hungrily from the jungle. We would cling to their belt buckle, flow in when they'd left. Make-do. Utilize.

"Take it easy," Jonathan says to me.

"Right. And the American extras are O.K?" I ask Binh for the tenth time. I still remember our crew of Europeans last year, during the first shoot.

"No problem, I told you. I arranged for them from the university. They're all one group of students."

"Any black guys?"

He hesitates. "There, the bus is pulling up. You can see for yourself."

I walk over, my feet squelching through the mud. It is raining softly but steadily. Binh and Jon pick up helmet-liners and clap them on their heads. The script and costume women are wearing floppy green NVA jungle hats and had draped themselves in plastic bags; they look layered and awkward as armadillos. Our sneakers or shoes are being encased in gobs of red mud that make you feel you are walking on a planet with twice the normal gravity of earth: more than the uniforms and dripping metal weapons, it sucks me back to the war.

The extras are climbing off the bus, smiling, blinking. They are the right age, haircuts good, but they're all white. Damn it, Binh, I think. They stand in the mud, joking with each other. I can't understand a word they are saying.

"Good morning," I say, to a tall blond boy. He looks at me blankly. Another, shorter, but with a square, All-American face—even, handsome features, very blue eyes, grins sardonically at me.

"Good morning, Vietnam!" he calls to me, in an accent I can't place.

"Where are you guys from?"

"We guys!" He seems delighted with the phrase. "We guys are from Russia. The former Soviet Union," he coaxes, seeing my face. "Your enemies. 'The little commie bastards.'" He laughs, calls out something to the others, who laugh also.

I stare at them. Oh shit, Binh. Russians.

We herd them into the small stone hut. The women have carefully kept the same fatigues the European extras had used, and I watch a large Russian put on a shirt with a faded black eagle, globe, and anchor on its breast pocket. Where did they manufacture jungle utilities? Some milltown in Massachusetts or Ohio or Tennessee, now gone to dot com businesses or economic depression? When we'd first arrived at Okinawa, we'd been given green dye for our white underwear, and when we went South we wore those and the regular Marine Corps utilities for a month or so, until the lightweight tropical utilities with the big pockets were issued. Utilities, as in utilize. After a time we got rid of the underwear, and wore only the baggy shirts and trousers, wore them for weeks on end, and they absorbed the fluids of the body, the cells of the skin. Until they became a baggy second skin for some kid, maybe from one of the milltowns that had made them and him. Stripped off when he'd been rotated or medevacked or killed. Kicked and spit on and ripped by a South Vietnamese major, enraged at being abandoned. Found crumpled in a warehouse after the NVA took Danang, and two troopers from the village down the hill here had entered the cool, tin-roofed cavernous space warily, AK's at the ready, and screamed in fright when they saw the legged and armed green shapes, like the ghosts of the old enemy. Pulled on now by kids from Moscow and Kiev, helped by the daughters of men who had once shot at the people wearing them. The long, strange trip itself. I may have said it aloud. The kid I'd taken for the All-American boy—he is completely dressed already, helmet, flak-jacket—raises his eyebrows and grins at me sardonically. "'Is that you, John Wayne?' he asks, 'Is this me?'"

*Full Metal Jacket.* 1987. Stanley Kubrick.

"Ex-scuse me sir," a boy calls to me. "Must we this?" He hefts a flak jacket at me.

"You bet." I go over and tap another Russian, who has put on his web suspenders backwards. "No," I say. "Nyet. Listen, Kubrick," I point at the All-American Russian, "how 'bout you interpret for me? Tell Ivan here these have to go the other way."

"No sweat, G.I." He salutes me, snaps his heels together, his eyes glinting.

One of the Russians is talking non-stop to the others, as if giving them instructions. He is big and has a broad, brutal face, accentuated by a crew cut. When he laughs, there is an edge of cruelty in it. He'll be Big Ivan, the steelworker from Pennsylvania. Who dies, I decide.

I get them outside, lined up in the rain. They look at each other, laughing. The Vietnamese nearby stop and stare, as they always did when they saw a squad of American soldiers suddenly standing on that soil.

Jonathan finishes positioning the cameras and comes over to inspect the extras. "They look mean," he says.

"They look like Russians. Or the fucking Serb army."

He grins. "We'll get them muddier. All you white guys look alike-la. Look, first shoot, I want them lying in the ditch," he points to the sand-bagged position, "facing that way, toward the hills. Get three or four of them to start there, run across there—by the bamboo fence; we're going to set off some explosions as they go by. They're shooting back towards the mountain as they run, but heading for the ditch, falling back. Everybody shooting like hell."

"Where are the NVA?"

"We got a special border police unit to do it. They're on their way."

"I'll muddy 'em up. The M-16s?"

"On the way-la." He turns. "Long! The M-16s."

I herd them over to the sandbag-rimmed depression. A machine gun is sitting on its tripod at one corner, completely exposed. I call over one of the prop men, and gesture toward a pile of sandbags, pantomime building a position around the gun. He nods. When I look back at the Russians, they are passing around a bottle filled with transparent liquid, drinking deeply, smacking their lips in a way you don't do with water. I sigh again. Everybody has to live up to his own stereotype.

"Listen, Kubrick," I say. "Tell them to put the vodka away and jump into that water." The center of the red-mud depression is sunken and has filled with rain water. "Tell them to wallow. You understand wallow?" I mime rubbing my face and chest with mud.

He snaps me another salute.

"You better salute, you commie bastard," I say, grinning at him.

"'Are they going to let us win this time, colonel?'" he asks.

*Rambo, First Blood: part II,* 1985.

"You bet."

One of the Russians whoops and lets himself fall backwards into the water. "Him," Jonathan says, coming back over. "That one—let's get him to fall like that during the attack." The other boys are laughing, jumping into the mud, throwing it at each other, smearing it on their faces and clothes. Passing the vodka. A dark haired boy with glasses, now opaque with mud, has taken one bottle and is pouring it into his canteen.

"Jesus," Jonathan says.

"Kubrick!" I call. "Let's get them lined up over here, get their weapons."

"This is my rifle, this is my gun!" Kubrick clutches his groin.

"That one speaks English?" Jonathan asks.

"In a way. He speaks war movie."

"How's that?"

"He seems to know lines from every Vietnam movie ever made."

Jonathan laughs. "Don't you love this, Wayne-oi? Is there anything better than this?"

We line them up, facing outward towards the northern slopes of the mountain, and Long, the quiet, ex-NVA sapper in charge of ordnance and special effects—that is, blowing up things—hands each an M-16. I show them how to keep their elbows up, not down into their waists, the way most people who'd never been trained tend to hold rifles when they are pretending to shoot. Long had loaded the weapons already. The tall blond boy points his barrel at me to ask a question, and Jon and I yell at him, at the same time, to keep it pointing away from us. We show them how to cock the rifles, use the safeties. They shoot off a ragged volley of blanks at the mountain. The smell of cordite drifts to me. One rifle has misfired, and Jon shows the boy how to clear it—he'd done two years of mandatory service in the Singapore army.

"Kubrick," I call. "Tell them to pull back the bolts twice, like this, then pull the trigger, make sure the rifles are clear." I demonstrate with my hands.

Big Ivan slams the butt against the ground, the shock cocking the weapon, as if he knew what he was doing. He catches me looking at him and grins disdainfully, then pats his chest. "Militar Russiya," he says.

"Animal Mother," Kubrick whispers to me, nodding at him. "He talks the talk, but does he walk the walk?"

*Full Metal Jacket* again. I finally realize just what he reminds me of. "I think he was in the 25th Platoon," I say. "Just like you."

He looks at me blankly. It was a term he hadn't heard in any movie.

The last time I'd run into the 25th Platoon was in what I'll call the Florida Bar, though it is located in a large Northeastern rust-belt city. I'd gone with two poets, Bill Ehrhart and Dave Connolly, ex-Marine and army. We'd been invited by a local poet and English professor who was doing Vietnam veterans, and by Country Joe MacDonald, who was making up for *Fixin' To Die Rag.* The bar was on the edge of the worst part of the city. It had a fenced, grassy 1/4 acre lot behind it, with a little pond and a shrine to the dead, over a miniature Japanese-type bridge. The shrine was the three figures of the Hart statue at the wall: black, white, and Hispanic G.I.s.

Inside, the smoke was thick as gauze. The walls were crusted with Vietnam war memorabilia—unit patches: 101st Airborne, 173rd Airborne, 1st Infantry, 25th Infantry, 193rd Infantry, 1st Cavalry, and more, mostly Army. There were helmets with green side out camouflage covers, flight helmets, baseball caps, and utility covers hanging in racks over the bar, and fastened around it were gold and silver flight crew wings, Combat Infantry Badges, airborne wings. There were 105mm brass artillery shell-casings, M-16s, K-bar knives, a collection of P38 ration can-openers on key chains, photos of young men in baggy fatigues holding weapons, a painting of a man in a suit touching his finger to the Vietnam Memorial wall which contained the ghosts of a grunt fireteam, one's hand outstretched, touching his. I think there were sandbags, though my memories of the evening are thick with gauze also. What else? The artifacts of a museum to perverse nostalgia. A shelf of Zippo lighters, one each, inscribed. *This Marine is Going to Heaven/He Served His Time in Hell. No Mission Too Difficult/No Sacrifice Too Big.* A naked woman bathing in a champagne glass: *When You Can't Be With the One You Love/Kill the One You're With.* One that got to me: *Too Young to Vote/But Not to Die/Too Young to Love/But Too Old to Cry.* T-shirts for sale, mostly POW-MIA: *You're Not Forgotten, They Still Wait,* and *Been There/Done That.* Above the door, large poster-photos of Westmoreland and Abrams, in tribute, and an equally large photo of Jane Fonda behind an anti-aircraft gun in Hanoi, not in tribute. I could say: it was that kind of place, but I'd never seen a place like it, except for a chain of theme restaurants built around the motif of a World War Two bomber squadron O-club. The idea of the thing: the Vietnam E-club Disney ride, only the animatronic figures might hurt you if you didn't take them seriously.

Some of the clientele were students from the poet's class. Most of the rest had dressed to fit into the décor and reinforce the myth. Ponytails, moustaches, black sleeveless leather vests, baseball caps with unit or Veterans' organization patches. *Vietnam Vet and Proud of It. Vietnam: If You Weren't There, Shut Up.* The experience had been anointed by the culture now. But I remembered when many vets would respond to the question of whether they had served in Vietnam by shaking their heads violently, as if to dislodge a word they felt imprinted in red on their foreheads.

"Oh Jesus," Bill said.

"Amen, my brother," said Dave.

Yes, I thought. But wondered if we were any different: three writers still living inside the war.

On the right side of the room were several overstuffed armchairs and sofas, the armrests black with grease stains, yellowish cotton erupting from tears in the upholstery. We got beers and struggled over, sat on one, the cushions sagging under us. Waves of noise from the small stage at the back of the bar blasted my ears, the music intertwining with snatches of war stories. You remember that seven-toed dink in Quang Binh? Swing with the Wing. What do they know, even the women and kids, booby-trapped, broken glass up the wazoo, we were right after all, lookit the boat people, we ran that orphanage, least we could do, heh-heh. Two tall lean men, both with black Bruce Springsteen goatees and baseball caps were sitting across from us. Connolly asked them what outfit they'd been in, found out it was his brigade. They began throwing names and places at each other. One rolled a dobie, lit it, inhaled deeply, offered it around. Hey man, be cool, his friend said. I fought for my country and I can smoke dope any fucking place I want, the first said. Bill seemed paralyzed, staring into the space directly in front of his eyes, as if, he'd convinced himself he was invisible. The only way to deal with this, I understood, was to be as drunk as possible as soon as possible. I began ordering boilermakers. The faces around me grew red-lit, saturnine, their edges trailing into smoke. There was a certain amount of border-blending. Country Joe got up and began the chant and the anthem. He asked everyone to give him an F, and they obliged, gave him the U, the C, the K, anything he wanted. Who were these people, the Woodstock generation or the boys from My Lai? Maybe that was the secret, no difference, we are all one.

> *And it's one, two, three*
> *What are we fighting for*
> *Don't ask me, 'cause I don't give a damn*
> *Next stop is Vietnam*

The mouths in the faces were all opening, lips forming the words. Bill had gone comatose. The grunts reflected in the black Vietnam Memorial, touching their brothers' hands on the outside, suddenly came through the wall, filed onto the lawn, into the bar, filthy, smelly, web gear dangling, weapons at the ready, stopped, looked around in anguish, and screamed, *We really can never go back to the World.* I suddenly understood what had happened, where I was. The plane had gone down on the way here. This was my afterlife. I was stuck forever in the Florida Bar. For my sins.

> *Ain't no time to ask us why*
> *Whoopee! We're all gonna die.*

A tall fat white man in a black sateen jacket with a Military Police badge on it was lecturing Ehrhart. "No, man, Westmoreland is so under-rated." A tall thin black man was standing in front of Connolly, swaying slightly, glaring down at him. His eyes were wrong. He put his hand in his pocket. I gripped my beer bottle. I saw Ehrhart do the same.

"You weren't there at all, you google-eyed freak, were

you?" the black man said to Connolly. "You never killed no little gook babies."

Connolly, it's true, looks, from some angles, like Mr. Peepers. It's deceptive. He's South Boston Irish and very tough, and he had been there enough to literally have his guts shot out. Blown off a half-track by a rocket-propelled grenade as he lay on the ground, watching his intestines spill out into the dirt, he'd seen an enemy soldier pop out of a spider hole inside the perimeter, between Connolly and the rest of his squad, their backs to him, and Connolly unable to move, unable to shoot, hardly able to scream, had to watch as the NVA killed all his friends. In the anti-war movement, he'd also been known for his fearlessness and the fierceness of his opposition to the war—he came from a family of IRA supporters and descendents, as well as from a family that was working-class and conscious of it in a way that probably no longer exists anywhere else in America as it does in Boston. At some point during the war, he became convinced that the working class was being slaughtered for interests not its own, and that, going through the villages, he felt like a British Black and Tan.

He wasn't, I wanted to tell the black vet, someone to fuck with. The man was glaring down at him. "You left me in the zone, you Jody motherfucker," he said. "Lying there and the chopper came in, and you took all the ofays and left the brothers behind. Left me bleeding. No Viet Cong ever called me nigger."

He pulled his hand out of his pocket. He had a razor blade in it. Bill and I started to rise, our hands clutching our beer bottles. The vet with the dobie took his arm, put the joint in his mouth. "Hey, bro' he ain't who you think he is. Come on down. Welcome home, man."

The man looked around wildly. "Saigon, shit, I'm still in Saigon," he muttered.

Ehrhart jerked his head around to look at him, a light shining in his eyes. "What outfit were you in?" he asked.

The man looked at him disdainfully. "The 25th Platoon, you honky motherfucker," he said proudly, naming a military designation that could never have existed. He walked off. A minute later, he was confronting someone else, across the bar, the razor in his hands.

"How did you know?" Connolly asked Bill.

"Shit, every word he said was from some movie or other."

"If you weren't there," the pony-tailed vet with the joint in his mouth said sadly, "shut the fuck up."

\*\*\*

We run the Russians all morning: dry runs, where they just pretend to fire, and then live-fire takes. The second scene would involve six extras crouching in the sandbag-rimmed crater; we'd use four M-16s on full automatic and the machine gun firing out at invisible NVA. To simulate mortar rounds coming in, Mr. Long, our ex-NVA sapper, has buried TNT charges packed in canvas bags—literally satchel charges without the shrapnel—a few yards out. I explain to Kubrick where everyone should go, ask him if he understands. He nods.

"All I ask of any man is he get his ass out in the grass with the rest of us," he says.

"*Rambo?*"

He looks offended. "*Hamburger Hill.*"

A small olive-green truck pulls up next to the stone hut where we'd dressed the boys. The back gate pops open, and Vietnamese in green pith helmets and fatigues begin jumping down, two, then four, six, ten—and it's suddenly clowns in the circus, an impossible number piling out of the tiny car, and it seems they will never stop, they would keep coming, overrun us; one horde to each truck, I've finally cracked the secret of the Ho Chi Minh Trail. Twelve, fourteen, twenty. Jonathan is laughing, shaking his head. "How the hell did they pack them in like that?" When they are out and lined up,

I see they are the right age—late teens and early twenties, though they look younger. As was right. But the green pith helmets are clean, and their fatigues look too new, pressed, bright. "No, don't worry," Binh says to me. "They're police, how do you say, for the border. We have old uniforms and sandals for them." He waves at the two women who are descending on the boys.

After the Vietnamese are dressed and armed, the Russians come over and the two groups switch weapons— AK47s for M-16s—and pose with each other. Looking at them, I feel nothing. It would have been more resonant, I think, if the G.I. extras were American kids—descendents of the combatants meeting to commemorate their fathers' war, instead of to kill each other. As it is, it looks like a ragtag group of Balkan guerillas from one faction or another, strangely reinforced by volunteers from the old North Vietnamese Army.

Afterwards, one of the Vietnamese kids, perhaps inspired by the clothing, begins practicing a low crawl through some concertina wire. I watch. It is the crawl of song and legend I'll later see demonstrated by a real sapper at Khe Sanh, though a real sapper would have come through the wire naked and greased and hung with bandoleers packed with plastique. But the kid knows what he is doing, has clearly been trained. Each move is deliberate, a series of short jerks, elbow, elbow, knee, knee, that flow together, and he moves over the ground as silently and smoothly as conscious water.

I bring Big Ivan and five others over to the pit, and get them set up.

"O.K, on 'action.' you're shooting over there—the NVA are coming right at you. Come on, translate Kubrick! After a moment, you'll hear the director yell fire! Don't hesitate, put your faces down. Later, we'll film you going over backwards. You got it? Kubrick, tell Ivan there if he keeps sucking that bottle, he's out."

Ivan shoots me a murderous look.

"Pay attention," I say. "You keep your head up, you may lose it."

I position them on the inside of the sandbags, their feet in the mud puddle behind them.

"Smoke," Binh yells, and Hung, our smoke machine, lights the tar mixture he's put into a basket on the end of a twelve-foot pole, and runs back and forth in front of the perimeter, swinging the basket. Binh yells something, and Hung runs over to camera A, lets the smoke billow in front of the lens.

"O.K.," Jon yells. "Roll A, roll B! Action!"

The Russians begin shooting fiercely, the echoes rolling off the hills. I see one of the M-16s isn't firing. The tall blond who'd asked me about the flak jacket raises the weapon and looks questioningly at the camera.

"Cut!" Jon yells. "Tell him just to pretend shoot-la. No matter."

On the next take, the boy points his rifle at the hill and pretends to squeeze the trigger, making shooting noises with his mouth. We can't hear him, but understand clearly, from the way his lips move, that he is saying "ka-chew, ka-chew."

"Cut!" Jon yells. "Tell him to stop that." I nod to Kubrick. When the firing began, he had seemed to freeze. He is looking off into the hills now, seeing who knows which war movie. "Kubrick," I say again, and he nods and yells something to the boy. The other Russians snicker. "Ka-chew, ka-chew," they chorus. Big Ivan looks disgusted. "O.K, one more time," Jon yells. "Roll A. Roll B. Action!...no, cut, cut!"

"Kubrick," I say. "He's still doing it. Tell him not to."

Kubrick goes over to the boy, puts his hand on his shoulder, looks him in the eye. "Yuri," he says gently, and then a stream of Russian, of which I understand, "Nyet," and "ka-chew." Yuri nods.

They're children, I think, and it isn't the thought or what it evokes so much as the words themselves that seem to freeze in my chest. The explosion catches me unaware; I didn't even hear Jon's shout. The shock slaps at me, and a few clods of dirt pelt my face and shoulders. When I turn around, Mr. Long is grinning at me.

"Missed again, you fuck," I tell him. I point my finger in his direction. "Ka-chew, ka-chew."

"Ka-chew, ka-chew," the Russians echo behind me.

When I look over for Kubrick, I see him squatting behind the umbrella set up over camera A. His hands are trembling slightly and he is very pale. "You O.K. Kubrick?"

"Never get off the fucking boat," he says.

It rains on and off all day, only letting up into a trailing mist that films dramatically, but chills to the bone. The Russians have poured the vodka into their canteens, and take long, gulping drinks whenever there is a lull in the shooting. It seems to make them happier, with the exception of Big Ivan, who becomes more and more surly. After Long's explosions, he and the others are to lay in the mud puddle and be dead. As Suong, the woman who had mentioned Salems to me, bends over Ivan, painting on blood, he clutches her ankle and begins groping up her leg. She smiles and shakes her head, as if to say, what can you expect from G.I.s?

"Cut it out, Big Ivan," I yell to him.

He sits up and glares at me. "Nyet 'Big Ivan.' Fyodor. You say—Fyodor." He thumps his chest again. "Militar Russiya. Good. Militar Americansky, Vietnam. Shit. *Scheiss.* You understand?"

"Lie down and be dead."

Kubrick says something to him sharply, and he lays down. He seems to obey Kubrick; they all do.

We shoot three more firefight segments, using both the "Americans" and the Vietnamese. For the last scene, everyone will be dead: a first for Vietnamese cinema, Binh tells me. In the past, they have never been permitted to show the dead from their side. We arrange them in the mud, smoke rising in columns from burning tires all around them: a G.I.

body here, a Vietnamese body there; sometimes only one, sometimes in clusters, sometimes entwined with each other. The reality would have been more like hamburger, but the smoke and mist and mud and fires; the uniforms and equipment and faces and where we are make it real enough, or at least representative enough, and for a second I have to turn away. They're children.

Big Ivan suddenly rises from the dead. He is shaking his head. "Nyet, nyet," he says, and shoots a stream of Russian at Kubrick. I look at him.

"He says it only looks like a movie. He says he was in the Russian army, he can tell you how to do it. He's drunk."

It is the first time Kubrick had replied to me in straight language. His voice is strained with a disproportionate anger. I start to say something, but before I can, Kubrick begins shouting. His face is pale in the mist, and I see his hands are trembling, as they had been after the explosions. The big Russian puts his head down, hangdog, like a scolded child, his size making it somehow more pathetic. He lays back down again.

"What did you say to him?" I ask Kubrick. He is still angry, very pale, his small, thin body trembling, and I think I see his eyes glistening. As I watch, he comes back to himself, shakes his head. "His ass," he says, "was never in the grass."

I look away for a second, at the field of the dead, Kubrick looking with me, still trembling slightly. Something occurs to me. "Chechniya?" I say to him. For a second, I think I see him flinch. Then he grins at me, his eyes bright, his face suddenly skullish in the gray light, and vigorously shakes his head.

## AN EXAGGERATED SPIRITUAL CRISIS

That evening I went to a seafood restaurant that sat on a bank over the Red River with Binh's mother, Phan Thanh Hao, his father, Nguyen Quang Hien, Hanh's father, Ngo Thao, and Do Quang Hanh, a journalist from the newspaper, *Lao Dong*, Labor. He was our host and had led us here through a series of twists and turns and alleys that seemed to have taken us deeper into some Hanoi of his heart that he wanted to present to me as a gift.

We ate fish and crabs and shrimp from the river and drank many beers. The filming with the Russians was still going on in the hills, but I'd hitched a ride back to Hanoi with one of the actors to make the dinner, clinging to the back of his Minks motorcycle for forty kilometers past dark, silent rice fields. The combination of the heat, of the beer, of a long, unsettling day in the mountains playing with armed, helmeted young men in jungle fatigues, of the journey by motorcycle and foot to this pocket deep inside old Hanoi, was blurring the edges of the evening, encouraging a sense of exaggerated significance that was reinforced by an awareness of who was at this meal with me now. That day on the shoot, I'd been struck by the sight of a wooden lunch table shared by young men in North Vietnamese Army fatigues and green pith helmets and young men in American jungle utilities and gear. Their clothing was tattered, filthy with sweat and mud, and some were sprinkled with prop blood. They joked with each other, passed the salt and pepper, AK47s and M-16s leaning against the chairs, like some hokey image of Valhalla, a reconciliation meal of the dead. The long table at the seafood restaurant where I was now echoed that table, and not only in size and shape. The diners sitting around it were the people their children were making the film about. And the people they weren't. The untold stories themselves. In the flesh.

Bich Hanh had somewhat based the character of Van, the poet "my" character was to spare, on her father. Ngo Thao had gone into the army after he'd freshly graduated with a degree in literature from Hanoi University. He had been a sergeant in an artillery unit that shelled Khe Sanh and the other American bases in Quang Tri province, where I'd spent some of my own war. Later, he had been made the political commissar of his unit, and had risen to the rank of Lieutenant Colonel. In fact, he was decorated with a citation which declared him "an eminent American-killer," a description, he told me, he'd stopped giving Americans when he saw it upset them. It upset me, I said. No, he meant it ironically, Hao explained. What the phrase really referred to was the way he would as a political officer, like his American counterparts, inflate body count. After combat, the bodies of the enemy were to be tallied: if only helmets, and other equipment were found—or rather seen, usually through high-powered binoculars. Each piece so spotted would be counted as one enemy dead. Five dead enemies would become twenty-five by the time the report reached the upper echelons: the higher it went, the more bodies would be added. Then the data would be divided per capita with credit given to infantry and artillery, in order to boost morale. That was how Ngo Thao received his title.

I still didn't see the humor, but I had long before adapted the attitude, in such situations, that we had all killed enough of each other to be at the same table. We had enough stories of our own about inflated body counts. What came into my head was the poet Bill Ehrhart telling me, a few weeks before, about his first kill: He had shot at a figure running at a distance of 400 yards across a paddy, and then found out it was an unarmed old woman. "Nice shooting," his buddies had commented. Since he was in the intelligence section of his battalion, he'd been able to witness the subsequent process whereby his victim was fictionalized first into an armed old woman, and then an armed male guerilla as the report of the kill went from platoon, to company, to battalion.

Ngo Thao and Do Quang Hanh were both combat veterans, though Hanh looked too young for it. I noticed he was staring at me, and smiled at him.

He didn't smile back. I asked him what was on his mind.

"It's a year past the twenty-fifth anniversary of the end of the war. In this country, we move on. Why do you keep writing about it? Are you so deeply affected? Or is it something you make up? After this much time, aren't you putting yourself into an exaggerated spiritual crisis?"

It was a phrase, I understood, he was trying out for the article he'd write. It wasn't a bad question, and a franker one than any journalist had ever asked me in Vietnam.

If he had asked me a few years later, when we'd become mired in a war that we'd gone into based on lies, self-deception, and a willed ignorance of the history, culture, and politics of the region that we'd entered, the answer about why I still wrote about the Vietnam war would have been obvious. But the scenario of a ground invasion and occupation of Iraq would have seemed like science fiction to me then, and Hanh's description troubled me.

An exaggerated spiritual crisis. Was I acting the role of the haunted vet, a writer—as I'd thought in that bar in Detroit—still living in the war? It wasn't that I hadn't asked myself the question before. The simplest answer to his question was that, like Ehrhart and Connolly, my companions in that bar, I wrote about it because I could, which created its own obligation. It was true, and a kind of cornerstone for me, but of course it wasn't that simple. Sometimes I feared that the war had become a definition I clung to because it *was* a definition, a defined role in the movie, and maybe one that gave me some credentials of masculinity in two professions—writing and teaching—my culture notoriously and grotesquely saw as effeminate. And my war hadn't even been that bad, not compared to the ex-NVA soldiers I knew, not compared to many Americans. I'd lived miserably and sleeplessly for a time, fired at people firing at me, but usually from a distance. The memories I held, the ones that lasted, were not of the violent and sudden erasures and dismemberments, given and received, that haunted so many people, but always of faces. Faces in the villages near Ky Ha. An old man I'd spoken to in high school French, asking me gently if I knew what I was doing there. The little girl who'd befriended me, and who I'd sworn I'd seen seven months later, in a whorehouse-bar. The girl in An Tan. Those faces and the faceless dead that day at Ky Ha, and the eyes of the wounded and dead we'd loaded into the choppers, pulled into the sky. Waste and betrayal. I had gone as a true believer. Many Marines did. The clichés about Marines had them as kill-crazy, obsessively macho, and I knew some like that, but as many more who were looking for a cause in which to subsume themselves, possessed of the same bent or quirk or genetic code that took people to the priesthood, or compelled them to board the freedom riders' buses. Afterwards, most of the vets I knew who went passionately anti-war, went to the streets or underground, were ex-Marines or ex-airborne. They wanted belief, had needed to give themselves to an institution wrapped around faith, embody it, be larger than themselves, and when they had become convinced that the war was wrong they had taken on the guilt of the institution, felt as if they needed to personally atone for it. With their bodies. It was the reflected and identical reverse of the feeling that had once made me volunteer to stick my body into the open hatch of a helicopter. The moment of my own turn against the war happened not during it, but afterwards, reading—I recalled precisely—Jonathan Schell on the village of Ben Suc, destroyed in order to be saved, on the artillery, air, and ground destruction of eighty percent of the villages in Quang Ngai province even before Calley set foot in the one the Americans misnamed My Lai. It was in Schell's statistics that I saw a context for my own experiences of how we regarded the Vietnamese: a burst of light that displaced me, made me nauseous, made me finally weep when I looked around myself in a crowded San Francisco park one day and saw all the people there as corpses draining into the earth, when I could see San Francisco as Hue. It was the same, exactly the same, as the feeling of sexual betrayal, the knowledge that love could no longer be trusted, the crumbling of the foundations of the world. In the end, I suppose, my obsession with the war, my sense of it being wrapped around me like a shroud I had to keep unraveling and re-raveling, my exaggerated spiritual crisis came from the same place Forrest had been: not from the horror of combat but from the sense of having touched an evil, a snake I knew I could find curled around my own heart as I'd once heard of one, a viper, found curled among the hydraulics of a helicopter; formed and coiled, not from the soul-sickness of murder but from the sickness of waste, from the sickness of finding the promise was a lie, from the heartsickness of seeing so much sacrificed for something so unworthy, from a frustration and rage at seeing so much of it, all the inflammable materials and disgusting badly smelt things, forbidden entry into the room.

I said none of this to Hanh. He was looking at me expectantly.

"I like your phrase," I said. "But not how you mean it. Not negatively. It's precisely what writers are supposed to do, isn't it? Create exaggerated spiritual crises? Pick or create the moments that let you see the real face of a person or situation? Look, I don't walk around traumatized by the war. And it's not the only subject I write about. But it was a spiritual crisis for my country, and I saw it, and I'm a writer. Just like Vietnamese writers these days seem to all be writing about the spiritual crises of losing the culture's values and uniqueness to consumerism, or the conflict between love and deprivation, and so on."

"O.K. But the Vietnamese books you bring to America are all about the war."

"No, not all. But, realistically, the war is what interests Americans in this country, if they get interested at all."

"Then at least you should have books by real combat veterans," he said. Thao nodded. They began to speak bitterly of a medal for artistic merit given to someone who was an entertainer during the war, rather than some of the writers who were veterans, or the war correspondents. They had one young man in mind, a writer-soldier who had died in Quang Ngai, and whose diary was returned anonymously by an ex-South Vietnamese officer who had taken it off his body. The diary was the most vivid and true account of the war either man had ever read—a limited edition of it had been published. "But there's no translation made of that," Hanh complained to me, "The real stories still aren't being told," he said, joining a succession of voices and faces, starting with Forrest's on the airplane, that all seemed to be telling me the same thing.

I looked over at Hao, who was concentrating on her shrimp. There are strong people at the broken places of the earth, Hemingway had said. Neither she nor Hien, her husband, who was kept out of the army due to a childhood injury, a poorly-healed broken arm, could be described as I had Hanh and Ngo Thao, as combat veterans. But neither Hien nor Hao could be described as unscathed by the war. The marriage of her son and Ngo Thao's daughter—the union of the poet and political prisoner's grandson and the ironic commissar's daughter—was in a sense symbolic of the new Vietnam, born from its own painful dichotomies. In her energy and ability, the strength that allowed her to survive what should have broken her and thrive and yet still forgive, so was Hao. The Vietnamese are too crowded together to hold grudges, she explained to me once, and wrote: "The national tradition is to forgive and forget. It is passed on into our subconscious from generation to generation, in lullabies, in folklore, and in ordinary life. For our country has learned to exist beneath a huge, culturally superior, and angry China...in our schools, we are taught that after the Chinese invaders were defeated, our kings had to take precious offerings to China and apologize."

Hao had educated herself while doing hard physical labor in factories and on road and canal construction crews, and now was a successful and altruistic woman who gave back much of her time, money, and skill to the country, translating literature, running an organization that trained drug and alcohol counselors and provided schools for rural children; who, in spite of everything, believed what her mother had taught her: "People aren't wolves." Ostracized, growing up under the bombs, helping to pull bodies from the smoking wreckage of her city while she helplessly watched her generation disappear, Hao had her own war story, one that could not to be shot in black and white, nor in brilliant color, but in muted colors, too subtle and complex, perhaps, to capture. The real stories still aren't being told. I knew that much of her life had been energized by the need to tell those stories, to allow the rest of the world to understand the complex suffering her country had undergone, the blunt needles that had mutilated its flesh in the struggle to reunite it.

The real war movie would not be a war movie.

Three million Vietnamese, from both sides, died in the war, and no one knows how many millions died afterwards, from wounds, from other effects, or how many still live imprisoned in their minds. Two years earlier I'd had dinner in the house of a woman who had been held prisoner and tortured by the South Vietnamese army; she could only speak of what was done to her by chanting it, in a wavering drone, her body rocking from side to side. My friend Nguyen Qui Duc, a South Vietnamese refugee, had seen his father taken prisoner by the North Vietnamese army in Hue: he had spent twelve years confined, nine of them in solitary confinement. Four years from this evening in the restaurant, the year before the 30th anniversary of the end of the war, I'd sit next to the beautiful guerilla Van Thi Xao, with her destroyed face, our trigger-fingers laced together, and next to Truong Thi Le as she rewove again and again the story of her family's slaughter, and stand next to a weeping Vietnamese-American girl who felt in the physicality of her body at that place the erasure of her father's history. The pain overlapped, and the need to claim a monopoly of victimization was, in the end, not a cry for justice but an excuse to continue hatred. "Don't you want justice?" Judd would ask of Truong Thi Le. But the violations of body and spirit were well-distributed. The country was reunified but it was sewn together with thorns. Every family had its epic tragedy, stories marked by suffering and humorous twists and strange ironies and terrible cruelties, by the most intense hate and love and heroism and cowardice. Everybody could sit at the table together. Everybody has a place there.

His goal, wrote Henry James in "The Tragic Muse," was to "create art as a human complication." What keeps me writing about the war, thirty years after its end, is not that I was in it, but the ever-dimming and ever-brightening hope that rendering the complexities of human nature through the resonance of story might just be the direct opposite of that ultimate lack of imagination, that ultimate lack of empathy, that, simply, allows us to kill.

# SCENE EIGHT
## The Elders:
## 2001-2004

# THE ELDERS

I met Tran Van Thuy two days after that dinner. I had felt, in many ways, that Vinh, the character based on the film-maker, not Van, should have been the character to whom John should have stood opposite and parallel; I wanted to see Thuy as another hovering witness, struggling to remember how it was, under all the pressures and temptations to remember how it was supposed to be.

Tran Van Thuy has an angular, squarish face, and a full head of long wavy hair, both of which don't so much diminish his body as allow one to see it as a bipod for his head and big eyes, magnified behind the two thick lenses of his glasses. We sat on the ironwood benches arranged kitty-corner against Phan Thanh Hao's living room walls, drinking green tea. He smiled at me.

"So we finally meet."

"I've heard a great deal about you," I said.

But what I was thinking about were the ways I could take his simple statement of greeting. I said that to him.

He nodded. "Where were you in the war?"

"Quang Nam and Quang Tri, mostly. What we called I Corps."

His eyes brightened suddenly, moving up and down my face so I could feel, or imagined I could feel, a physical brushing of my skin. I didn't drop my gaze. "Then, yes—so we finally meet," he said. "I spent much time in Quang Tri. After I went South."

I smiled. "Do you know, that term? It was the same we used. Probably not all Americans, but the Marines who were on Okinawa. When we got orders to the war, we called it 'going South.' It meant the same as to you. Going to the war. Going to death."

He nodded, still staring. "When were you there?"

"Sixty-six to sixty-seven."

"Ah." He nodded. "Yes. I was there then. What was your duty?"

"Most of the combat duty I had when I was in Quang Tri was as a helicopter gunner."

He gasped, brought a hand to his chest, as if touching his heart. It was very demonstrative for a Vietnamese man, and took me by surprise.

"I hated the helicopters so much," he said excitedly. "I was so afraid of them. I took film of all the other American aircraft—A7s, F15s—I'd stand with my Bolex and get them as they were coming right at me. But I couldn't do it for the helicopters. I could only run and hide. The noise and wind of them coming down. The creatures in them, staring down, like insects, chasing us, smashing us—I'm sorry." He reached across, his hand not quite touching my face, but waving over it, as if it were a way he could see the features more closely, ascertain their reality. "You have a nice face," he said, shaking his head in amazement. His eyes were suddenly brimming, and then so were mine. We didn't speak for a time, and Hao, silent also, refilled our cups. It was a moment I'd had before, meeting people in Vietnam I could have killed, and who could have killed me, and discovering I liked them. But I hadn't reacted this strongly for a long time. What I'd usually say, and what I said then to Thuy, was that I was glad I hadn't killed them, and they would, mostly, say the same, and we would mean it. But what I'd feel, and what I felt now, was not relief but a sudden grief, whose concrete image was a row of muddy boots and whose core was built around the word that had come to my mind when I'd seen the abandoned equipment and helmets in the storage room. Waste.

"I have a friend," I told him. "You may know her—the

writer Le Minh Khue. She worked on the Trails during the war, told me the same thing you just did. How, of all the aircraft that attacked them, she hated and feared the helicopters most. I always wonder if I'd flown near her then. Shot at her. It was how close we got that bothered her. As you say. The B52s, the other aircraft, were completely... inanimate. But there is something alive, insect-like, about the helicopters, machine-like, mechanistic, and yet flesh...some merging. And if—as you say—you glimpse the crew, all helmeted, armored...I don't know. There's a point in the film where the Vietnamese commander calls the Americans 'bugs' to be wiped out...the way we called you gooks..." I realized I was babbling, the English getting too complicated, and tried to pull my thoughts together. "In the scenes I've read in the script that involve the guy based on you, 'Vinh,' we, the Americans, if we're shown at all, it's like that, as a sort of relentless, inhuman force..."

"Yes," he said gently. "But as you say...you did the same. It's realistic, isn't it?" He stared at me in silence for a while. "There was only one way we could see each other." He smiled wryly. "There was only one way I could show our own side also. I shot so much film I couldn't show. At the time, I thought it right. I thought of my film as a weapon to help win the war."

"And now?"

"I regret that I couldn't show all the human damage. That was my true duty as a film-maker. And you? What did you see as your true duty?"

"My duty? Then?" The question took me aback. I'd been thinking of John and Vinh, my need for a symmetry of vision between them. But it wasn't a consciousness I could claim at the time. "At first to be there. Later, to not be there."

"Ah."

"How close did you ever get to us?" I asked him. "How close to any of the American soldiers did you come?"

It was something that I'd once asked Khue, though I was

unsure, then and now, why it meant so much to me, except perhaps for how his words had made me feel towards him at that moment; the gift of grief that Khue had allowed me also. *I can attach faces to grief and love and pity...* Tim O'Brien had once written of his work.

Thuy measured the distance between us with an outstretched arm. "This close," he said. He'd had to hide in a spider hole when American troops came unexpectedly to a village where he was filming. (When I traveled with him in 2004, one of the places we took the NYU students was the Cu Chi tunnels, that famous network that had been dug in the area where the American 25<sup>th</sup> Infantry Division fought. Thuy showed us in a tunnel there how he'd have to go in the hole, which was so narrow he had to extend both his arms out straight above his head, like a man about to be held up or arrested). When he'd emerged from the hole, he had found himself staring at the back of a G.I. shaving with the soap and water in his upturned helmet. The two of us sitting together now, he said, had brought back that memory. The film was doing the same, he said, bringing back so much. As if the character, Vinh, was a shadow at the edge of his eyes that turned his vision, shifted it to an angle that allowed him to see, to focus into clarity, the mob of memories that always pulled at the periphery of his vision.

We were at Hao's with Ngo Binh Long, a Vietnamese-American scholar who had also been an advisor and angel to the film. Hao, Binh and Hanh and, later, Jonathan were there. The film was to have been completed by this time, and in fact a forty minute segment had been shown at Cannes. But the kids weren't happy with it. They had several ideas, but first they wanted us to see it as it was now, even without the new battle scenes done with the Russians. "We value," Binh said, "the advice of the elders."

I tried that term on for a time, as Hanh started the video tape. I liked the implication of calm wisdom it called, though I didn't feel ready for its other implications. In any case, Binh and Jonathan, Hanh and Peggy, had had the vision, had been told over and over they couldn't do it, had gotten it done. What did they need us for—four old-fart elders, *lao gia,* shaped by the war?

Though that of course didn't stop us from speaking when Hao pressed Stop. It was, after all, our war, our territory they were entering, wasn't it? The film was beautiful, cinematically. And often seemed to work. Yes. But the flashbacks were confusing and sometimes too abrupt, Thuy said. And some of the stories and characters really aren't developed enough, I offered. Both Van and Vinh—the character based on Mr. Thuy—were the points from which we get the story: Vinh through his filming and voice-over and Van, as it should be, through his diary. But that's never really exploited, and the scenes where his wife finds him at the battlefront and his commander gives him leave seem unrealistic. Even if that really happened, it seems unreal, and besides, it takes away from Van as a witness. Do you need that? Near the end, the tank breaking through the presidential palace gate in Saigon, Long added—the scene looks artificial, and the image has become such a cliché. Do you really want the end to include it? You'll alienate, Thuy said, millions of overseas Vietnamese with that. And May, I said. I've always hated that name. You have a character named "lucky" in a war movie; everyone knows he's going to die. And the way he does here, running across the palace lawn, on the last day of the war, and then dramatically clutching his chest and saying, "I'm lucky.." That's awful. Also there's not enough death, Thuy said, nodding. The dream scene of the dead in the forest is good. But this unit has been at war for seven years—you haven't shown enough of the dead... You must show more of the dead.

Afterwards, there was a silence. We all sipped our little cups of green tea.

"But of course it looks wonderful…" I started.

"Yes," said Thuy. Long nodded.

Jonathan raised his hand. "No, that's why we asked your advice. And we agree with much of this. But what did you think of your scenes with Quang Hai?" he asked me.

Here we go—the end of my acting career. "I looked somewhat artificial in the restaurant scene," I said cautiously.

"I think, besides what you have already said," Binh said, "what bothered us the most are those scenes set after the war. As Thuy said, the story keeps stopping, it gets confused. And using the young actors in makeup with the veterans…"

"It doesn't look right," Hanh said.

The three elders were all nodding.

"We will talk over everything you said," Binh said. "But we also have an idea for the, how do you say, structure of the film. We want to film several new scenes to replace most of those with the young actors and the elders. Instead we will have the real veterans speaking to each other, about their experiences or feelings. Real stories. Mr. Thuy and the real Lam." He nodded at me. "You and Mr. Thuy at the same tree where we filmed with Quang Hai…"

"A scripted dialogue the two of you will write," Jonathan said to me, "but you'll do it as a natural free-flowing conversation—the script just kind of a reference point. These scenes will be like a frame to hold the rest of the film. It will let people know this is all real. That's what we feel is missing. We want it to be entertaining. But we don't want people to just see it as movie real—we want them to know it is about real pain, real…" he looked at Thuy "…bodies."

We were silent. I looked at Jonathan. It got you, I thought. You came to do one thing and the country turned you around and you found that what you wanted was quite different than what you thought it was. It wasn't the first time that had happened here.

"I don't know," Long said.

Thuy remained silent, his eyes closed behind his thick glasses.

"There's a risk you take," I said slowly, "that you can

lose your audience when you put into their minds it's one kind of narrative—a movie, a story, a fiction—and then suddenly switch to another, to, as you said, frame the imagined stories with real people and events. You may break the magic, the dream of the story. If I did it in a book, ran together fiction and nonfiction, I might confuse readers—no one will know what to call it."

"Yes," Jonathan nodded, and he and Binh and Hanh grinned at each other. "We talked about that. Everything should be done in certain ways. Everything is laid out. No surprises. Spotless. Labeled. Like Singapore. Why not—it works-la. Does what it's supposed to do-la. Makes everyone happy. But what did you call us in that thing you wrote—the kids? Nothing we did was supposed to happen anyway. So we thought, the hell with it, we'll do it how we want."

They just wanted to include everything, I thought. That's all. I knew they would fail, as we all failed. I knew they had to try.

*Out-take: The Eye of the Nation*


Queues of jagged white rocks break through the soil here and there, the spine, the people say, of the dragon that sleeps under the village, protecting it. Vinh looks down at the cluster of thatched houses from the hill, pans the Bolex over it, looking for a shot. What is wanted, he knows, are not dragon bones but peasant-heroes with rifles slung over shoulders, hands on plows; old women who have given all their sons and daughters to the revolution, their faces carved to nobility by age and grief; young women smiling as they squat and carve punji stakes to skewer the American invaders or puppet troops. And so on. He is tired of all of it, too tired even to think why he is tired. It isn't that such people don't move him, still, after all these years. He's seen the price they pay. He knows their sincerity. A sharp, sour taste rises in his mouth. He's been feeling bilious, his stomach bloated. The villagers have fed them simply but well, one old grandmother even finding some soybean milk sweetened with sugar for him, a taste that brought him back to his childhood. But for weeks, before coming here, he'd eaten with the soldiers and the young girls in the Youth Volunteer unit he'd been filming: nothing but manioc and tapioca from the little fields they'd cultivated in the Truong Son Mountains, sometimes nothing but roots. Maybe that's all that was bothering him. His stomach. But a vague image is flapping insistently in his mind, its very nebulousness making him feel more ill at ease. It focuses into a flag being waved atop a captured bunker, and then, yes, he does know what has been bothering him. He hates doing reenactments. Prides himself on being there. He is the eye of the nation, he's been told, and he has come to believe those words described what he wished to be. Too many of the other correspondents relied only on reports, official communiqués, but he was always at the front, with the people doing the killing and dying. Everyone knew his combat footage was the best, only rarely re-staged. Yes. But it had been a significant victory and he had only been notified afterwards, when the soldiers had already buried their comrades. So he'd gone to the scene, and positioned the filthy, weary men here and there, like arrangements in a composition. Told them to run this way and that, as the sappers set off harmless explosions. There had been a beautiful young private who he'd placed on top of the heap of bloody, riddled sandbags in front of which so many had fallen, and he'd instructed the boy to raise and wave the national flag triumphantly, though in the real battle the commissar had forgotten or misplaced the flag. No matter. It was all as formal and choreographed as a classic dance. He'd comforted himself with the thought that at least the soldiers he'd used had actually been in the fighting at that place. But then, weeks later, a sergeant had told him that the beautiful private had been a coward who'd refused to advance, pissed himself in terror. He told Vinh this as if the cameraman could take back film once it was exposed, had the power to change a vision that met so many needs, as if it wasn't too late to tell the truth. Now the image of that boy had been seen in movie theaters in Hanoi and all over the North, and in War Zone B, in the South also, flickering onto parachute silk backdrops set up in caves and tunnels. Sanctified now and forever by his, Vinh's, film.

Well, he thinks, and so what? At least the boy would be of some use now. He was a good-looking boy, and in war, Uncle Ho had said, even poetry must become a sword. It was a lovely thing to say. A nicely balanced dichotomy. No. He shakes his head, rejects his own cynicism. Maybe it is just gas. His sour gut. In the unit where he'd picked up his two escorts, May and Manh, there'd been a commissar who checked the size and amount of the men's turds after their bowel movements, to be sure that everyone ate equally, everyone ate small. In the spirit of egalitarianism, Manh had said to Vinh. Film that, cameraman. In war, even shit becomes a sword.

He hears a noise, swings the camera around, catches Manh running up the hill toward the banyan tree where he is standing. Manh is wearing a peasant's black cotton shorts and shirt, unarmed. Vinh centers him in the lens, then sweeps right and left, wondering where May is. His two guardians. He usually prefers to go on assignments alone, and he is valued enough now that headquarters lets him. But when he'd asked to do this assignment, filming Liberation Front villages and fighters operating right under the noses of the Americans in Quang Tri, headquarters had assigned two liaison scouts to accompany him. He doesn't mind. They are repatriated Southerners and knew the area, the people. May is a village boy who has somehow maintained a sweet naivete through five years of war, though his name, "lucky," sent a chill through Vinh when he first heard it: it is a name like a target, a name in a bad war film given the character everybody knows will die. Who in their right mind, in wartime, would name a child "Lucky?" Manh, standing in front of him now, reaching out a thin, fine hand to push the camera lens down, is the Sardonic Jokester. He'd been an art student in Hue during the anti-Diem Buddhist riots, had fled North after the massacre of students and monks. His home village is near here.

And he is, Vinh sees, very agitated.

"What is it?"

"Please come quickly. Don't you hear the helicopters? We've gotten intelligence that the Americans are going to sweep through here. Please, elder brother, put the camera down." Vinh has raised the lens to capture Manh's face, his eyes, at the moment he brings the news.

"How long..." Vinh begins, but as if his words have called it, he hears, at a distance, the sound of helicopter rotors beating the air. His blood freezes. An image: locusts eating his flesh, opens in his mind; it always does when he knows the helicopters are coming. They are the insects of insanity. We should keep going, get out into the paddies and jungle,

Vinh thinks. But he demurs to Mahn, follows him at a run back to the village. But he demurs to Manh. May is waiting for them behind Mrs. Ninh's house. "Quickly, elder brother," he says, his forehead wrinkled with the tension of the responsibility he feels about Vinh. He leads them to a row of cactus fencing a small cornfield, grasps one of the cactus ears, and lifts. A small section lifts up: the plants are in a foot of soil over a bamboo trap door. He sees that flame-retardant *trung quan* leaves have been woven to the underside of the trap. The hole is deep, but the space inside looks barely large enough for one person. Manh wiggles in, gestures for him to follow. It isn't, Vinh sees, a tunnel, simply an opening in the earth, wider at the bottom than at the top. A grave. He stops, but May firmly presses his hands against his back and pushes him. He has to raise his hands above his head to fit into the hole. He goes in heavily, on top of Manh, who grunts, expelling breath rich with fish sauce into Vinh's face. The narrow shaft opens into a slightly wider hole at its bottom. Vinh looks frantically back over his shoulder and sees May closing the trap door after himself like the lid of a coffin.

It is immediately pitch black. Over it, he can hear the beating of locust wings. His heart scrambles in his chest like a trapped animal. Like himself trapped in this hole. As if he is a heart. He can hear his own blood pulsing in his ears, the sound as loud and hollow as the wooden fish drum at the village pagoda. His draws his knees up to his chin, clasps his hands around them. May and Manh must be in the same position, though he can't see them. There's no room otherwise. The earthen walls push on him. The surrounding darkness itself has turned to hot, wet flesh and is pressing at every inch of his body, sealing his closed eyes. Over all of it is the terrible whirring noise of locusts, and now he can hear explosions, a crescendo of firing, the crackling of straw on fire, even the hum of bullets. The affairs of the earth continuing unabated, heard from his grave. Or waiting for him outside his womb. Here, in the belly of the dragon. His clothing, the thin shirt and shorts, takes on a weight of its own, adding another layer he begins to find unbearable. The buttons on his chest feel red hot as they push into his skin, his waistband squeezes his painfully bloated stomach. He lets go of the camera, useless in this dark. The three of them are pressed together, flank to flank, like fish steaming in a pot, gasping, and he wonders if they would breathe up all the air in this little space. Their breaths are already filling it; they must be by now breathing mostly carbon dioxide, he thinks. The heat and the closeness and airlessness are panic itself, but what he fears most is the blackness, pressing at his eyes, taking away that sense, so that he is blind. He can't stand the thought. He begins scrambling for the lid, trying to straighten his knees, stand, but May and Manh both grasp him, pull him down, hold him. Manh, he thinks it is Manh, is forcing something into his mouth, a hard wooden tube—bamboo. He sucks at it, drinks the smoke tainted air as if it is mothers' milk. He is in a kind of trance. Manh—or was it May?—slides the tube out of his mouth, the joints of the bamboo segments scraping his tongue, passes it to the other man. The third fetus, Vinh thinks dully, his brain heavy and soft and fibrous in his skull. The soul transmigrates into the body of the baby waiting to be born. Pressed into the womb, would the soul's past life reel past its inner eye in flashing images, frame after frame, fast forward, reverse? All the strips and squares of film seen and forgotten or left cut into strips in the jungle mud, the floor, would they be pasted back together for a final viewing? Would he be allowed to reincarnate or would he be sent to one of the lower hells? Wombed and tombed now, he knows the answer. He knows what he has seen and what he has refused to see. The dragon hisses his, Vinh's, own secrets into his ears. He knows he is bloated with lies. He is the eye of the nation and he has chosen to be blind. He has refused to see and now he is blind. He has allowed his eyes to create lies. The images the fetus plays on the screen of its interior vision are the price of lies. The lies are here with him now, in the dark, stinking and rotting, stillborn, they are his twin brothers, embracing him.

What does he see? He had once seen and captured the

long-suffering nobility of that old woman's face, her hands work-callused and capable, her life a paean of self-sacrifice. But he had closed his eye, capped his lens when it began to open a soul so battered with grief it had shrunken cowering into a small corner of the woman's mind, screaming behind her blank eyes, the stoic mask of her face. He had stopped filming, had stopped seeing, but now he sees the wreck of her daughter's body, flesh hanging in strips from it as if it has turned to paper, and the heap of bodies he saw and refused to see in Tay Ninh, a pile into which her sons might have been incorporated, Vietnamese and Americans, naked and entangled as lovers, as more than lovers, since so many of the parts themselves were separated and mixed, brown arm growing from white neck, white leg over brown chest, as if Heaven had torn this flesh in a rage, presented it, said begin again. Reincarnate. He tries again to rise, but his twins clasp him, hold him down tightly to themselves, in his pool of blindness, and outside fusillades of shots and screams and explosions that tremble the flesh of the earth and move into him, but he doesn't care, he just wants to push out of the blindness he knows now he has chosen for himself, he needs to see, to see.

May and Manh hold him down. He thinks he passes out though it is hard for him to judge. In the close darkness all lines and borders are invisible. He dreams the taste of sweet soybean milk in his mouth. He is back in his boyhood home. In the courtyard some *ylang-ylang* trees stand near the well and a pile of red tiles. He is walking Black Dog. As he walks, he thinks of a film he will shoot about Black Dog. He knows in the film Black Dog will run into a thicket and squat like a black frog. He releases the dog knowing it will follow his vision. Instead, it shoots off in the opposite direction, towards a brown and white heap of something on the other side of the courtyard. It is a dead cow. Black Dog clamps its ear between his teeth, growling in his throat, and begins gnawing at it. He pulls the dog away, screaming, "It's dead." They walk on and suddenly there is a tiger lying on the side of the road. He is confused. It shouldn't be here. There is no tiger in his film. It gets up, bares its fangs, growls, and Black Dog leaps towards it. Someone is shaking his shoulder. "Elder brother, wake up," he hears Manh whispering in his ear, and he feels the segmented bamboo being pushed into his mouth again.

He doesn't know how long they have been here. The sweat of their bodies has glued them into one flesh and into the flesh of the earth around them. In the darkness the dream clings to him longer than dreams should, staining into the air. He can't see. He is suddenly, again, very afraid: what if the darkness has taken his vision permanently. He and the two other men are gasping, and when he puts the bamboo into his mouth again, no matter how hard he sucks, nothing comes through. If they stay here, he understands, they will die. He rises a little and pushes gently against the underside of the trap door, peers out of the crack he's made.

He drinks in the air. The light stabs his eyes. He closes them, opens them a crack also, like the door. Like the slowly opening iris of a lens. The world of the living slowly sorts itself out for him. To his left, a house. To his right, a dead water buffalo, on its back, its head twisted towards him, its fly-crusted eyes looking at him reproachfully. In front of him, seen through a lattice of cactus, is an American. His back is to Vinh. He has hung a small mirror from a peg on the corner-post of a house and is shaving. Vinh thinks: have I been underground so long this has become America? He can see a small image of the man's face, lathered, in the mirror. A bamboo table in front of him; on it, Vinh sees as the man moves to the side, is an upside-down helmet into which he dips the razor. The American's back is covered with brown spots, and here and there, patches of coarse hair. He seems to be conducting an orchestra. A madman, shaving among smoldering ruins, as if to create an order only he could control.

He closes the lid. May or Manh is pulling him, clutching him, whispering to be cautious. But he has to get out. The hole now seems to be squeezing in on him, pulsing. He grabs his camera with one hand, pushes the lid up and over, opening the opposite side, just a crack. He slides through silently, keeping his chest and belly on the earth, keeping behind the cactus fence, then helps May and Manh. As each face peers at the crack, Vinh puts a finger to his lips. The three men lay on the ground. There is no wind and the stench of the fire and the dead buffalo is still thick in the air.

Manh begins crawling towards the ditch at the end of the cactus row. Vinh sees what he has in mind—the ditch runs to a field of elephant grass. If they can make that, they can get into the forest. He crawls, stops, crawls again, inch by inch, as slow as a shadow. Glancing up, squinting, he can see himself reflected at the bottom of the American's mirror, inching like a slug. The American shuts his eyes, tilts his chin up. Vinh crawls further, watches himself disappear across the bottom of the mirror. He hears the noise of rotors.

He freezes, feels hot spots burn on his back and neck like premonitions of bullets. Hears a burst of firing, sees rounds flying up at the aircraft from the other side of the village. Perhaps to distract the helicopter from him. The famous guest, he thinks. Angry and sickeningly grateful at once.

The three men leap to their feet and run into the jungle. Like three red-assed monkeys, May will say later. Vinh trips, flies through the air, lands, rolls, runs on. He looks down, sees he is intact, though bleeding from a dozen cuts.

They hide that night in a small cave. The Americans are all around them. In the morning it is silent, and they move through the jungle until they come to a small stream running down the center of a valley walled by high hills. As if coming to a silent agreement, they strip off their filthy clothes and slide into the water. Three heads grinning at each other. A foolish move, Vinh will think later; there must have been an observation post on the hill. He hears a series of dull thuds and then watches, stupefied, as the water down stream erupts in huge geysers that seem to march straight at him. Out, May screams, and he has time only to grab his Bolex and the three run naked and zig-zagging as the earth around them shatters in a series of explosions. They make the tall grass just as three F-14s—one for each of them?—roll out of the sky, dive towards them, strafing the area to their west. They run and Vinh pictures them doing it and laughs hysterically as he zigs and zags: three naked men hunted and shelled and strafed by the entire might of America.

They crash into the jungle. There is a lull now. A great silence descends. He sees the lens of the camera is shattered. Yes. It is what he deserves. His brain seems shattered also. Like a mirror. He sees the reflecting shards of it, a thousand fractured images, all gone. He picks it up like a broken child killed for his sins. Bad karma from bad actions. He remembers now what had run through his mind as he was embraced by the walls of that hole. The omissions of his past life. He was the eye of the nation and he refused to see. Now each image he had refused to press into the eyes of those for whom he was seeing lay imprinted on a shard of the shattered lens. They cut into his brain. It is right. His camera is a weapon and in war, poetry must become a sword. But his camera was the eye of the nation and he should have pointed it at that political commissar in Quang Tri who checked the turds of the men in his company to make sure no one was eating too much, an image as true of the war as the men who had run without hesitating into enemy machine-gun fire from that outpost near Dong Ha, and truer than what he'd done to them afterwards, when he'd made them mere extras in a flag-waving, piss-pants lie. Yes, he thinks dizzily, it is right now that his lens is cracked, but he refuses to let go of the camera and Manh is shaking him and making him move.

What do you see, cameraman? The dragon asks him.

He sees a grouping of *ylang-ylang* trees in a small cool courtyard, an unexpected tiger lying next to them.

He sees the hairy back of a beast who is peering into a mirror, so intent on its own face it can't see what is right behind it.

He sees, when he looks closely enough, under the patches of beast hair, the vulnerable, freckled, skin of humanity.

He sees again every death of body or soul from which he has turned his camera, his sight, away.

"It's all right, elder brother, there, there," May says gently. "Don't you know my name means lucky?"

The green locust of a helicopter whizzes by overhead and he points his shattered camera up and in it captures, as if through the thousand-faceted eyes of a bee, the equally insectoid face of the American framed in the hatchway, peering blindly down through the dark lenses that cover his eyes.

*John's fingers touch the butterfly trigger. A butterfly touch.*

# DRAGONFLY

*A butterfly touch.* While John, in using what is after all the correct name for the trigger of his gun, *butterfly*, is perhaps unconsciously trying to suggest the fluttering uncertainty of his own press on that metal, and while Vinh might reasonably see the helicopter as *locust*, if we look at it now, darting here and there as it flies away, we—in our need to tie all of this fragmented, confusing, seethe of stories and images and insects together—might do well to think instead of *dragonfly*. An insect sometimes called *devil's darning needle* or *snake doctor* or *snake feeder.* The helicopter swings South, perhaps to pick up some prisoners and a snake at LZ Crow, to follow without joy the curves of Highway One, flying like a frantic dragonfly attempting, like that highway itself, to knit it all together, knit the splintered, bisected country. Just as the invisible Trail it would fly over, the enemy's Trail, bombed and cratered, was trying to do, the girls on it laboring under the canopied trees that hid them from John's eyes, smoothing it whole with their hands, hearing the noise of the rotors, the wings of the dragonfly, beating above them as if to remind them of the price of the legend they already feel they are living. The helicopter flies South. It is still flying. It never stops.

\*\*\*

The year before I returned to Vietnam with my son Adam and the New York University film students, Adam had made his own pre-graduation journey to Burma, where my wife

.

210

comes from, and to Vietnam where—he perceived correctly—I came from. He had preceded me that year to many of the places in Quang Tri, Hue, and Quang Nam we later came to in 2004, and so was able to guide us knowing, as he did, the more recent geography of places I had been during the war. The son leading the father.

He also knows the story of Jim Childers, the boy who had died in my place. We had flown out of the helicopter base near the mountain, and Jim had been shot landing on another nearby hill, and so Adam had gone to Marble Mountain and made his own tribute, climbing up to one of the formation's summits, saying a Buddhist mantra an old lady at the base of the hill had taught him, and lighting some incense, as he later wrote, in the hope that his "muttering, stumbling thank you was enough for a man I had never met."

Marble Mountain, *Ngu Hanh Son* in Vietnamese, is really a series of five marble formations, honeycombed with caves that are used as Buddhist shrines. During the war one cave had been a secret Viet Cong hospital: we mostly left the mountain alone, since it was used as a religious shrine, even though we knew we were occasionally mortared from that area. That hospital cave (its roof now holed by an American bomb that burst inside in 1969, when the facility was finally discovered) was no more than a mile or two from our camp, and closer still to Charley Med, the field hospital where Childers had died.

The area was of course completely changed, except for the basic topography of the two mountains that had bracketed us: Monkey Mountain to the north, Marble to the south. Driving down from the Hai Van pass, we followed a wide clean road that bordered the beach where the Americans had first landed in 1965. In the war, the area along the road out from Danang stank with raw sewage, and was heaped with ramshackle, makeshift cardboard and tin shacks, filled with desperately poor refugees displaced from the countryside: further on, the road to Marble Mountain that ran past our camp had been a narrow strip of mine-cratered, buckled concrete that ran through sand flats, empty except for the occasional flattened-beer-can shack. When I'd been on a trash detail for a time, we'd had to take a six-by truck filled with trash from the base up to a dump near the base of Marble; we'd had to travel fully armed, guarding those scraps of used tin, plywood, shredded canvas, cans and wire, which would soon be salvaged by the horde of Vietnamese waiting at the dump for us: the debris of one world becoming the props of another. One of the men with us liked to take boards or filled cans and fling them at people walking or riding their bicycles on the road. Cut it out, I'd told him, and then, to make sure I wasn't accused of being a gook-lover, I said: we ride the same way every day, and I don't want to get shot.

Now, in 2004, that same road was smooth, wide and well-paved, its sides crowded with housing, some of it quite new and prosperous-looking. The helicopter base itself, I understood, had been taken over by the Vietnamese army, but I could see none of it. It had been, to my relief, swallowed, and whatever memories I had I kept inside myself, inside the air-conditioned bus, away from the students. I'd already let myself be vulnerable more than I'd wanted on this trip, and that road and that base was no longer visible, and let it stay that way.

I was in that mood when we got to the mountain, *Ngu Hanh Son.* The journey suddenly seemed too self-consciously ritualistic; my son had come here last year by himself; that was enough. The fact that our ascent would be filmed, part of a movie, made it worse, made it performance.

"I don't think I'll go up," I said, when we'd walked to the base of the mountain. Adam looked startled, then nodded. Helen Contino, the NYU administrator along on the trip, said, "No, don't go, Wayne. Not if you don't want to." The students, looking at me, murmured in agreement.

"No," Judd said. "You have to go."

My feet started moving, as if by their own accord. "Don't do it," Helen said angrily. "You don't have to." I waved at her. "It will be all right."

The first part of the climb was up a series of steep steps carved into the stone. The temperature was in the nineties, with the humidity at a nearly equal number. After a time, I felt my heart start pounding irregularly, felt dizzy—the same symptoms I'd felt before being hospitalized just before the trip. I shook my head angrily. You have to go. Judd's words had somehow been internalized.

We went into a cave, and then clamored up, using hands and feet, over broken rocks, through a narrow enclosed spout. When we came out of it we were on the top of one of the formations, at the highest point.

It was the other side of the mountain from the helicopter base; the side we never saw. To the east was the sea. To the west was the long valley of the Song Yen, gridded with rice fields—the site of many battles—and on its edge I could see Hill 327, where Childers had been fatally shot.

I turned away from the students and Judd, and looked at it. I had told myself I wasn't going to show any emotion here, be the weepy vet for the camera. It wasn't working out. I wasn't ashamed of the unexpected tears in this place, or particularly surprised either. There had been a river of tears under the thin ground of this journey, and I no longer knew when it would grow too thin and the river would break through. In Hanoi, when Phan Thanh Hao was showing us the damage of the war, at one point she had broken down and cried. Later, mortified, she said she was a teacher; she should never let herself become un-objective like that. Look, I had told her confidently, the best teaching is when you let yourself be vulnerable, when you allow your students to see what something costs and means. But it was advice I didn't now want to take myself. I didn't want this mourning that was shaking my shoulders now, the sobs I was trying to keep bolted in my throat, to be a show, a lesson; I wanted it to be private, grief for the sake of grief, for the sake of the boy I mourned, for all that I mourned.

Then my son came over and put his arm around my shoulders and passed, for me, into his manhood. And even in the sudden joy of that revelatory moment, I cursed the careless elders who had stolen such moments of light forever from Jim Childers.

# THE BANYAN TREE

Thuy and I walk down the dirt path atop the flat ridge of a berm sticking out of the paddies. Ahead of us, a man is putting rice into a wooden threshing machine, turning a crank. In the paddy below, a boy raises water from one lock to the other in the paddy canal, dipping a canvas strip suspended between four ropes into the water, pulling the ropes apart so the strip rises, tautens, snaps the water out into the next level. It is harvest time, and the rice fields are alternating patches of glowing green and gold, all the way to a horizon marked by black jagged mountains. The only other break in the expanse in front of our eyes is an ancient banyan tree, its roots webbing a cleared, slightly raised circle of soil, an island in the midst of the fields. Moad Jeffri and the camera crew are over to our right, some dozens of yards away on the road, and so walking and speaking we can create the illusion that we are just two men, veterans of the same paroxysm that has formed our lives, coming to some peace with each other.

The banyan is perhaps sixty feet tall, with a thick, complicated trunk and gnarled, muscular roots jutting out of the earth all around it. It is the same location where I'd shot a scene with Quang Hai, as "John" and "Van," earlier in the year: the diary-writer showing his country at peace to the man who'd given back his diary. Jonathan had spotted the tree when he and Binh were driving through the area, scouting locations, and it had fascinated him. I understood why. The villagers we spoke to said that the tree was nine hundred years old. I'd read that, in the old days, such ancient and huge trees in the midst of fields were considered attractive, because of their shade, to various spirits, and children were cautioned to avoid them, particularly around midday. I'd used that idea and such a tree, transplanted to Maryland, in a novel once, and coming to this tree I had the sensation not of déjà vu, but of having written a path I hadn't known I would actually follow. It had happened before: scenes described from what I thought was imagination appearing in front of me years later, as if they had been remembered backwards. The location lends itself to that kind of mysticism, and even though there doesn't seem any prohibition on kids coming to this tree at midday—there are a number gathered around us, including a boy on the back of a water buffalo—it is easy to see it as an abode. The trunk, when you touch it, is smooth and very hard and cold but also somehow damp and fleshy. It has the ancient, faintly mossy smell of pagoda stones. A cone of coldness emanates from it, so that, in the midst of a day when both the temperature and the humidity are in the nineties, putting your face near the tree is like sticking your head into an air-conditioned room.

Thuy and I make ourselves as comfortable as we can on the arched backs of two dragon-shaped roots that rear up to stool-height from the ground. These are nearly at the border of shade and earth: beyond it are the rice fields that go on until they stop at the line of dark mountains. We smile at each other, like two men about to hear a secret each knows can only, finally, be told by the other.

## AUTHOR'S NOTE AND AFTERMATH:

When I began to write this book, I went back to some stories I had written not long after I'd gotten back from the war, and that were published, in 1973, in the anthology *Free Fire Zone*. They are linked stories, and my original intent was to develop them into a novel. But after the anthology came out, for a number of reasons, I found I didn't want to write about Vietnam, and I gave up on the novel. I took *Free Fire Zone* from the shelf now, for the first time in years, because I wanted to jog my memory for several of the scenes I was writing. But when I looked at the first sentence of the story "Medevac:" "Standing by for medevacs, he always had the feeling he was being centered in a movie camera," I realized that story was waiting for this book.

*Song of the Stork* was completed in 2001, just before the events of September 11th; a bad time for a war movie that was, after all, about peace (*The Quiet American,* also scheduled to be released, was, at the time, held back by Mirimax for the same reason). That year, *Stork* was shown at the Cannes Film Festival. In 2002 it appeared at the Taormina Film Festival in Italy, and at the Milano Film Festival, where it won the award for Best Feature Film. It was also shown at the Montreal World Film Festival, The Goteburg International Film Festival, and the Bangkok International Film Festival. Distribution rights to the film were sold to European and Japanese distributors, and, in 2003, as a new war movie began in Iraq, to an American company. It is generally felt in this country, though, that, among other things, the movie's mixture of real people and events and actors acting out imagined events is not audience-friendly.

The film opened in Vietnam in December, 2002, at the Hanoi Opera House.

The documentary shot by the New York University students was being edited at the time this book was finished.

WAYNE KARLIN served in the Marine Corps in the Vietnam War. Since that time he has returned to Vietnam several times and has worked for reconciliation between the two countries. He has previously published six novels: *Crossover, Lost Armies, The Extras, Us, Prisoners,* and *The Wished-for Country,* and an earlier memoir: *Rumors and Stones.* As the American editor for Curbstone's "Voices from Vietnam" series, he has edited and translated fiction by writers from Vietnam. In 1995, he co-edited with Le Minh Khue and Truong Vu *The Other Side of Heaven: Post-War Fiction by Vietnamese and American Writers,* which the Asian American Press said "Veterans from both sides of the war are hailing as a major contribution toward international healing." The anthology, *Love After War: Contemporary Fiction from Viet Nam,* which he co-edited with Ho Anh Thai, was chosen by *The San Francisco Chronicle* as one of the best 100 books of the year in 2003. He is a professor of language and literature at the College of Southern Maryland.

# CURBSTONE PRESS, INC.

is a non-profit publishing house dedicated to literature that reflects a commitment to social change, with an emphasis on contemporary writing from Latino, Latin American and Vietnamese cultures. Curbstone presents writers who give voice to the unheard in a language that goes beyond denunciation to celebrate, honor and teach. Curbstone builds bridges between its writers and the public – from inner-city to rural areas, colleges to community centers, children to adults. Curbstone seeks out the highest aesthetic expression of the dedication to human rights and intercultural understanding: poetry, testimonies, novels, stories, and children's books.

This mission requires more than just producing books. It requires ensuring that as many people as possible learn about these books and read them. To achieve this, a large portion of Curbstone's schedule is dedicated to arranging tours and programs for its authors, working with public school and university teachers to enrich curricula, reaching out to underserved audiences by donating books and conducting readings and community programs, and promoting discussion in the media. It is only through these combined efforts that literature can truly make a difference.

Curbstone Press, like all non-profit presses, depends on the support of individuals, foundations, and government agencies to bring you, the reader, works of literary merit and social significance which might not find a place in profit-driven publishing channels, and to bring the authors and their books into communities across the country. Our sincere thanks to the many individuals, foundations, and government agencies who have recently supported this endeavor: Community Foundation of Northeast Connecticut, Connecticut Commission on Culture & Tourism, Connecticut Humanities Council, Greater Hartford Arts Council, Hartford Courant Foundation, Lannan Foundation, National Endowment for the Arts, and the United Way of the Capital Area.

Please help to support Curbstone's efforts to present the diverse voices and views that make our culture richer. Tax-deductible donations can be made by check or credit card to:
Curbstone Press, 321 Jackson Street, Willimantic, CT 06226
phone: (860) 423-5110   fax: (860) 423-9242
www.curbstone.org

IF YOU WOULD LIKE TO BE A MAJOR SPONSOR OF A
CURBSTONE BOOK, PLEASE CONTACT US.